THE REVENUE ZONE

The Ultimate Playbook for the Next Generation of B2B Sales, Marketing, and Predictable Revenue Growth

TOM BURTON

D1075960

Creator: Tom Burton, Revenue Zone Media
Title: "The Revenue Zone: The Ultimate Playbook for the
Next Generation of Sales, Marketing, and Predictable Revenue
Growth"

ISBN: 979-8-9858439-0-3

To my wife, Lorin. Without her love, support, and encouragement, this book certainly would not exist.

CONTENTS

INTRODUCTION

In Marshall Goldsmith's bestselling book, *What Got You Here Won't Get You There: How Successful People Become Even More Successful,* he explains the necessity of changing your mindset, habits, and behavior if you hope to reach the next level of success in business and in life—even if your current mindset, habits, and behavior have already made you very successful.

In the world of B2B sales and marketing, this premise has never been more true. Without a doubt, what got you *here* will not get you *there.*

As I will explain shortly, I learned the hard way that, despite thirty-five years of experience in B2B sales and marketing and building successful businesses, I could no longer rely on the strategies and techniques that had worked for me up to this point. I had to rethink everything and change my mindset, habits, and behaviors. I had to develop new strategies and techniques to continue thriving in the changing world of B2B sales and marketing.

I also discovered that I was not alone. In talking with friends, colleagues, and even prospects and customers, it was clear that what *got us here* in the sales and marketing profession generally will not *get us there*. That is exactly why I decided to write this book.

Whether you are just starting your business career or are a seasoned sales and marketing veteran, this book will provide you with a precise playbook for making consistent sales and driving predictable revenue growth over the next decade and beyond.

Before we continue, let me take a minute to introduce myself. My name is Tom Burton, and you most likely have not heard of me before.

I started my career (yes, over thirty-five years ago—ouch!) as a software engineer after graduating from the University of California, Santa Barbara with a degree in computer science. My interest in technology and software, however, stretches all the way back to my high school years in Long Beach, CA in the early 1980s. When I was a junior in high school, I was lucky enough to be accepted to a selective early morning computer programming class, and every morning I would get up and go to school early so I could attend this class and write computer programs on their newly purchased Radio Shack computers. I knew then that computers and software technology were in my future because they combined my interest in science and math with my interest in inventing and building interesting things. I can still remember the thrill of creating my first Blackjack program on those Radio Shack computers and the upset of losing it all when my sister spilled water on the 5 ¼ inch floppy disk it was stored on. Oh well…

After graduating from college, I went to work at a startup software company (way before that was the cool thing to do), and over the next 10 years, I helped the company grow from a handful of employees to hundreds of employees and offices all around the world. During that time of explosive growth, I transitioned from software engineering to the operational side of the business. This gave me experience in all aspects of our company's sales and marketing efforts and led to me spending three years in Europe setting up our operations there.

Since then, I have been involved in founding, growing, and

selling multiple software companies as well as consulting with startups and Fortune 500 companies alike, and even running my own digital marketing agency for a period of time.

I have worked with many sales and marketing organizations in many different industries ranging from software to safety products. I have developed sales methodologies, funnels, and playbooks, created extensive digital marketing campaigns, and helped build sales and marketing organizations.

Today, I am a co-founder of LeadSmart Technologies, a unique and rapidly growing CRM software company, and continue to consult and advise companies on their sales, marketing, and go-to-market strategies.

After all these years in business, I had seen it all and then some—or so I thought…

As I look back over my career, it is clear that what got us all here and what made us successful as B2B sales and marketing professionals has, at the same time, been creating a larger and larger chasm between us and our prospects and customers. Many B2B buyers will do anything possible to not have to deal with a sales representative, not share their business email address, and remain totally anonymous as long as possible. The following data points from a 2020 report by Gartner[1] on the future of B2B sales further spotlight this conflict in the changing business landscape:

- B2B buyers are spending only 17% of their total buyer journey with sales representatives.

- A sales representative has roughly 5% of a customer's total purchase time when you consider that purchase decisions involve many different suppliers.

- 44% of millennials prefer not to work with a B2B sales representative.

- Millennials are generally twice as skeptical of salespeople as baby boomers.

Going one step further, Gartner also reports that "33% of all [B2B] buyers desire a seller-free sales experience"[2] and that "70% of the buying process is completed before a buyer interacts with a sales organization."[3]

---

[1] Adamson, Brent and Toman, Nick. "5 Ways the Future of B2B Buying Will Rewrite the Rules of Effective Selling," Gartner (August 4, 2020).

[2] "The Future of Sales: Transformational Strategies for B2B Sales Organizations," Gartner (2020).

[3] Albro, Scott. "The Buying Experience: The Most Important Thing in Sales and Marketing," Gartner (August 21, 2019).

Wow!

Unfortunately, this desire for a "seller-free" sales experience can also hurt the prospect by forcing them to rely solely on online information and data, which can be confusing and overwhelming. Confused and overwhelmed prospects rarely become paying customers.

Clearly, we need a better way that enables buyers and sellers to be "on the same page" and working together, not against each other. We need a new system, approach, and playbook that:

1. Creates trust with the buyer and a willingness to talk with our sales teams.

2. Provides the buyer the right information, at the right time, without overwhelming them or creating unnecessary confusion.

3. Enables the buyer to essentially become an extension of our sales team and an ambassador for our company.

4. Results in consistent sales and predictable revenue growth in our business.

The philosophy, strategies, and techniques presented in this book (which I have named the Revenue Zone System™) have been developed specifically to provide a solution to the challenges associated with these four points.

I have been utilizing many of the components of the Revenue Zone System in my businesses and with my clients for many years. However, the complete Revenue Zone System that you are about to discover really only came together recently, and I have been working diligently to test and refine it so that it can be used and applied to any B2B business. I have been fortunate to have the support of a great team and the businesses we have worked with.

In particular, I need to make a special shoutout to my business partner and co-founder at LeadSmart Technologies, Kevin Brown. Kevin and I have been friends since kindergarten (yes, that is over fifty years), and Kevin has spent his entire career working with companies that sell indirectly through third-party channels such as distributors and dealers. Kevin's expertise, help, and support have been instrumental to the creation of the Revenue Zone System and adapting its principles to industries that sell through partners and third-party channels.

Like the subtitle says, I believe this book is the ultimate

playbook for the next generation of B2B marketing, sales, and predictable revenue growth. That is not hype or overconfidence. If you learn and apply the strategies and techniques in this book, you can radically increase sales, create predictable revenue growth, and build strong relationships with your prospects and customers.

In addition, to help you with your implementation and adoption of the Revenue Zone System, my team and I have created an in-depth and continually growing online Resource Center at therevenuezone.com/resources. Details on how and when to use these free but very powerful resources are included throughout the book.

Please take a moment now to visit the Revenue Zone Resource Center and register to receive notifications when new resources are added or updated.

Now let's enter the Revenue Zone!

CHAPTER ONE

A SHIFTING BUSINESS LANDSCAPE

I was attending my first live, in-person meeting in over a year. The room was filled with board members, investors, and executives all there to review our goals and priorities for the rest of the year. The first item on the agenda was discussing revenue and sales projections for the quarter and the rest of the year.

I launched my PowerPoint presentation and dove into a description of our sales "pipeline." I reviewed how many prospects we had at each stage of the funnel, the probability of each one closing, and their potential revenue value. My slides were sharp, and the team seemed pleased and impressed with the presentation.

When I was done, one of the board members asked how confident I was about the pipeline and sales projections I had just presented. The palms of my hands suddenly became clammy. I tried to stay calm, but the anxiety I felt inside was new and unwelcome. Before, whenever someone had asked me why I was confident that my predictions were correct, I could always give an informed explanation based on evidence. This time though, I didn't feel so sure. I basically gave the board member an answer that equated to, "Just trust me."

It occurred to me right then that I had no idea if what I just presented was even close to accurate. Worse yet, I realized that my revenue projections were more of a guess than a reliable estimate. Things had been changing in our business, and my usual methods of predicting revenue growth were no longer relevant.

This uncomfortable event caused me to realize that things hadn't just changed in our business—they had shifted in huge ways across *every* industry. And this shift didn't just require normal adjustments. No, it required serious evolution; it required a transformation in how we look at marketing, sales, and customer acquisition. We had to fundamentally rethink how we generate revenue in our businesses.

In spite of my assurance that my numbers would be reliable, I became acutely aware that my understanding of and approach to sales and marketing needed a major overhaul. My career depended on me quickly figuring out why I had lost confidence in my projections and, more importantly, what I could do to fix them.

So I did what any adventurer would do: I embarked on a journey of discovery. I looked everywhere for others who were seeing what I was seeing and feeling the same anxiety I was. I listened to podcasts. I browsed websites. I watched countless videos and attended way too many webinars.

At first, I was at a loss. But as I sifted through all the information I had gathered, two common themes emerged:

1. **B2B buyers today want to buy products and services the same way that consumers do.**

2. **Traditional B2B marketing and sale techniques do not align with how B2B buyers now want to buy.**

I also discovered that some businesses were rising above the rest by *allowing the buyer to control their own journey.* These buyer-curated journeys were literally turning prospects and customers into high-performing salespeople and brand ambassadors for these businesses. Does that sound too good to be true? It did to me until I saw the evidence.

I was thrilled by my discovery! That's when my background as an engineer kicked in: I knew I needed to somehow translate these principles into a system that could be successfully used not only by me but by anyone.

In this book, I will share with you the Revenue Zone System™, which enables you to align your marketing and sales processes with the modern buyer's journey and turn your prospects and customers into your own high-performing sales team. It's time to enter "the Revenue Zone" (cue *Danger Zone* by Kenny Loggins).

WELCOME TO THE REVENUE ZONE

The Revenue Zone is a place in the buyer's journey where a prospect is *seriously considering spending money on your products or services.*

This does not mean there is no other competition, and it does not mean the prospect is not seriously considering buying from others. It does not even mean the prospect is ready to close and make the purchase.

What it does mean is that the prospect is at a place where they are seriously considering doing business with your company.

For a prospect to enter the Revenue Zone, two things must be in place:

1. **The prospect must have a fairly high level of demand for your product or service.**

2. **The prospect must have a reasonable level of trust in your company.**

The natural question to ask is, "So then, how can I get a steady stream of prospects into the Revenue Zone quickly and efficiently?" Thankfully, I have an answer.

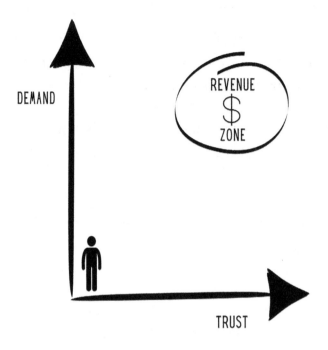

The Revenue Zone Criteria

YOUR YELLOW BRICK ROAD

Have you ever seen *The Wizard of Oz*? In this famous movie from 1940, a young girl named Dorothy is in trouble. After smashing a house into the Munchkins' mortal enemy, the Wicked Witch of the East, the mythical Munchkins help Dorothy find her way to The Wizard by following an unmistakable yellow brick road.

I am going to set you down a path that is equally helpful and that will—dare I say "magically"—lead you and your prospects right into the heart of the Revenue Zone. No, I won't ask you to smash any enemies with your house. Yes, you'll find a treasure at the end. But first, I want to help you know if this epic journey is a good fit for you and your business, whether it be a small startup or a huge Fortune 100 company.

IS THIS BOOK FOR YOU?

Have you ever been worried or concerned about how your business (or the business you work for) will make more sales, generate more revenue, and get more customers? Have you ever had a moment of anxiety, like I did, in a sales presentation or creating a sales forecast? Have you ever wondered if there was a better way to guide prospects through the buyer journey that yields both incredible results and pertinent data?

The truth is that sales, marketing, and revenue leaders all over the world still have the same mandates they have always had:

1. Generate consistent sales and revenue.

2. Achieve predictable revenue growth.

The strategies and techniques outlined in this book have been predominantly developed for business to business (B2B) sales, marketing, and revenue professionals as well as C-level executives who are looking to capitalize on the disruption of the buyer's journey by turning market changes into a competitive advantage and a growth accelerator for their businesses.

Now, you may be asking, "Can the Revenue Zone principles be applied to B2C?" Yes, much about the Revenue Zone can be adapted to B2C marketing and sales, especially for larger-ticket sales, but most of the strategies and techniques discussed in this book are more tightly aligned with B2B.

MY PROMISE TO YOU

If someone had said to me a few years ago, "Hey, I know how you can turn your prospects and customers into your primary sales team," I would have been skeptical. But now I know this is not only possible but essential. You too can get your prospects and customers to use the power of word-of-mouth to evangelize your product to their colleagues, friends, and family.

So, what's my promise to you? I promise that if you take the time to learn and apply the Revenue Zone System (RZ System), made up of the Revenue Zone Matrix™, the Yellow Brick Road™, and the Revenue Expansion Flywheel™, you will have the power to convert your prospects and customers into your company's primary sales force. I will teach you a system that is counter to many of the sales and marketing techniques you have been taught. You don't have to take my word for it, either. Work your way through this book, learn how to build your own RZ System, and see if it doesn't do everything I promise it does.

Now, before we get into the *how* of this system, we need to rewind a bit. Why did the time-tested, old-school sales and marketing techniques of the past suddenly stop working?

That's a trick question. Actually, they didn't "just stop working." They've been declining in efficacy for decades. If I had been more observant earlier, I could have read the signs and known what was happening well before getting into that predicament with my sales presentation.

THE SIGNS I MISSED

When I first started researching the cause of the shifts in buyer sales preferences, I assumed that most of the changes were rooted in disruptions created by the recent pandemic. However, after further research and discovery, I realized that the key drivers behind these shifts were in place well before COVID-19 hit. While they were certainly amplified and accelerated by the pandemic, major shifts were already taking place in the business world.

VIRTUAL BUSINESS

Prior to the pandemic, most people thought of "Zoom" as something you did in your car. But during the pandemic, we saw a massive shift toward using programs like Zoom, Microsoft Teams, and Google Meet. Any type of software that enables virtual meetings and conversations between employees and their prospects, clients, or teammates suddenly soared in popularity.

While older business models emphasized the importance of in-person meetings, conferences, shows, and other live events, this shift to virtual business highlighted the benefits of not having to travel out of town—or even leave home.

Many companies have embraced virtual business as a means to attracting qualified employees and talent regardless of where they live. In addition, businesses are reducing travel costs and increasing productivity through the use of more and more virtual meetings. "Digital first" has become the mantra at many companies whether a buyer or a seller.

Of course, there will always be a need to have offices and have in-person interaction. However, virtual business is here to stay, and this trend was already taking place, especially in some industries, well before the pandemic.

THE PRIVACY-FIRST PARADIGM

In the previous decade (2010-2020), marketing and sales

strategies and techniques were often facilitated by easy and inexpensive access to third-party data (i.e., data related to what your customers and prospects were doing online, the websites they were visiting, and the Google keywords they were searching for). The usage of an email or telephone number was governed by a small number of privacy laws, and most of these varied based on where the business was being conducted.

In the current decade, society's privacy paradigm has and will continue to change rapidly. Depending on when you are reading this, it is likely that easy and inexpensive access to third-party data related to your prospects and customers will be difficult or even nonexistent. Web browsers may not allow third-party tracking cookies at all, and collecting emails from opt-in forms on your own website could be very difficult. Privacy laws and legislation will also be more numerous, stricter, and will dole out greater consequences to violators.

As more people and companies conduct business online, the issue of privacy will continue to be at the forefront of policy discussion. In addition, as we will explore in much more detail in later chapters, current prospects want to remain anonymous until they are ready to engage with your sales team or fill in an opt-in form to access content on your website. As a result, our marketing and sales techniques and strategies must embrace and leverage a new, privacy-first paradigm.

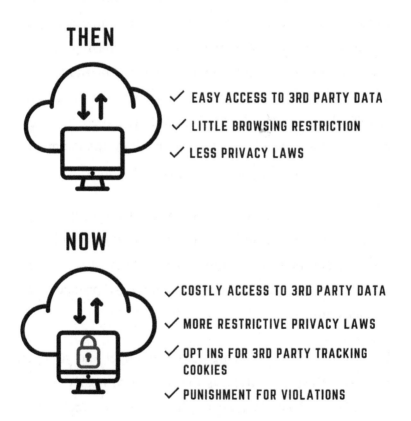

The Shifting Privacy Paradigm

SHIFTS IN B2B BUYING BEHAVIOR

One of the key takeaways of my research was that B2B prospects and customers want to buy the same way that regular consumers do. As consumers, we are accustomed to doing our own research when considering making a purchase. We have also embraced online purchasing through online retailers like Amazon and other e-commerce sites. We don't want to engage with a salesperson unless we absolutely need to, and, if it is needed, we expect the salesperson to be more of a guide or consultant than someone who tries to use high-pressure sales techniques.

More and more, B2B buyers are expecting a similar "digital first" experience and want to be in control of their own research and their own buyer journey. They also want the opportunity to research, shop and purchase products and services online.

In addition, B2B buyers are getting younger and younger. Forrester Research suggests that by 2025, nearly half of all B2B purchase decisions will be made by tech-savvy millennials who have little patience for dealing with traditional sales approaches.[4]

---

[4] McBain, Jay. "Global Marketing Content Credibility Study," Forrester (Q3, 2019).

THE PERFECT DISRUPTIVE STORM

As I stated a few pages ago, we still have two primary objectives as sales and marketing professionals: *make consistent sales and achieve predictable revenue growth.*

We want to accomplish these objectives by having control and visibility over our prospects' and customers' buying journeys. We want our prospects to engage with our sales teams when we want them to. We want to know when prospects are considering our products and/or services. We want to know who they are. We want to build strong personal relationships with our prospects and customers, so we know what they are thinking and considering.

However, *our desires are outdated and have been permanently disrupted.* Ignoring or complaining about these disruptions will not change the situation. If we want to generate sales and achieve predictable revenue growth in our businesses now, in this decade, we need to approach sales and marketing very differently.

Though the pandemic did accelerate the adoption of virtual business, it didn't create the demand for it. It also didn't create the demand for stricter privacy laws—people and governments did. And given our buying behavior as consumers, it isn't a surprise to find out that most B2B buyers want to be in control of their own research and buying decisions. Together, the pandemic and the pre-existing demand for privacy and virtual business created a perfect disruptive storm of sales and marketing changes.

This perfect disruptive storm has changed the landscape of business as we know it. Now it's time to look for alternative strategies that don't depend on in-person sales meetings, third-party data collection, or sales-controlled buying journeys. The best way to forge a new path through the disrupted business landscape is to create a new one altogether. That is why I propose building out your own Revenue Zone process, complete with your very own Yellow Brick Road, using the framework and techniques presented in this book.

Without further ado, let's dive into the Revenue Zone System, its components, and how they will change the way you think about sales and marketing forever.

Chapter Summary

- I discovered (the hard way) that traditional sales and marketing actions and forecasting were outdated and ineffective.

- I embarked on an in-depth research quest to understand what was occurring and why. According to my findings, business buyers want to behave more like consumers when buying and traditional B2B sales and marketing tactics do not align with this desire.

- The Revenue Zone introduces a unique system and approach for generating consistent sales and achieving predictable revenue growth with today's B2B prospects and customers.

- The disruptors driving this new world were taking hold prior to the pandemic but were amplified and accelerated by COVID-19.

- Virtual business is here to stay.

- Privacy is a huge concern for both individuals and businesses and will continue to be scrutinized by lawmakers and legislators.

- B2B buyers want to be in control of their buyer's journey and expect a "digital first" experience.

- Millennials will make up most of B2B buyers by as early as 2025.

- The Revenue Zone System will help you build a Yellow Brick Road that leads prospects into the Revenue Zone as efficiently as possible.

- The Revenue Zone System will help you make consistent sales and achieve predictable revenue growth into this next decade.

Discussion Questions

- Have you observed in your business that traditional sales and marketing techniques are becoming less effective and results more difficult to forecast?

- How has the perfect disruptive storm changed the landscape for your business?

- Which of the disruptors discussed in this chapter is having the most impact in your business?

- What would you like to achieve with the Revenue Zone System?

- Do you think your business is a good candidate for the Revenue Zone System?

- What are some of the ways you hope the Revenue Zone will improve your ability to make consistent sales and generate predictable revenue?

CHAPTER TWO

WEATHERING THE DISRUPTIVE STORM

In 1997, my wife and I started our first business together (we were just married at the time). Our company revolved around a unique software product that we had developed that helped companies manage complex technology projects without having to hire expensive consultants. The software was well received. We were signing up customers left and right, and we were even awarded a patent on the core technology behind the software.

In early 1998, we decided that we wanted to grow the company faster and possibly bring in venture capital to help fund our expansion, so we worked out an agreement with an experienced colleague whom I had worked with in my previous company to be our advisor and mentor in the process. So far, so good! Right? Unfortunately, we made a big mistake.

As it turns out, the agreement we signed with this person was extremely lopsided in his favor. It was legally sound (we had our lawyer review it before we signed), but it contained terms and conditions that gave this person way too much control and veto power on key business decisions. Long story short, he ended up blocking a deal with a very reputable Silicon Valley venture capital firm that was ready to invest millions of dollars in the business. The business never really recovered, and we limped along for several more years with slow growth.

So, why am I telling you this? The reason we got into this lopsided agreement was that we had no practical instructions or best practices to guide us in structuring a fair agreement for bringing on a minority partner into our business. We acted based on our instinct and, to a degree, emotion rather than on clear guidelines or "rules." And, as a result, we paid a very large price for our inexperience.

In order for you to weather the perfect disruptive storm we discussed in Chapter 1, you need to be in a position where you do not have to rely on instinct and emotion like my wife and I did in our business. As a result, in this chapter,

I am going to introduce three Revenue Zone "rules" that will provide a foundation for weathering the storm and for successfully implementing the strategies and techniques I will discuss in upcoming chapters.

I am also going to introduce some mindset shifts in this chapter that we as marketing and sales professionals will need to make if we are going to be successful with this new approach to generating consistent sales and driving predictable revenue growth.

Let's get started by reviewing the three Revenue Zone rules as they relate to the three elements of the perfect disruptive storm.

THE VIRTUAL BUSINESS RULE

One of the biggest benefits of virtual business is productivity and flexibility. "Digital first" is the policy many companies now default to before considering travel or even local, in-person meetings. In many cases, you can work from anywhere that you have an internet connection, and for many companies, coming to the office every day is a thing of the past.

Of course, there will always be trade shows, conferences, live events, and even in-person meetings from time to time. However, these have now become more the exception than the rule.

I totally understand that this new world of virtual business can be very scary, especially if your sales and/or marketing approach currently revolves around shows, conferences, and in-person meetings. I remember a client whom I worked with a few years back in my digital marketing agency who, when I first met them, relied entirely on trade shows to reach qualified prospects. Fortunately for this client, we helped them build out other marketing channels before the pandemic hit, but I am sure many other companies were not so fortunate.

So how do we as sales and marketing professionals deal with this new world of virtual business? The answer lies in Revenue Zone Rule #1.

RULE #1   **Become a valued consultant and guide for your prospects and customers.**

Transitioning yourself away from being a "salesperson" and toward being a valued guide and consultant enables you to build and maintain strong relationships with your prospects and customers without the need for in-person meetings and interactions. It also enables you to help your prospects gain clarity and "make sense" of their online research. Let the prospect and customer be in control of their own sales process (more on this in a minute) and be ready when they need guidance and support. If you are viewed as a trusted consultant and guide, you will successfully build strong relationships with your prospects and customers virtually. And, when you do meet in person, those meetings will have greater impact and results.

"DIGITAL FIRST" IS NOW THE DEFAULT.

THE PRIVACY PARADIGM RULE

In addition to privacy concerns, the fact is that your prospects want to conduct as much research on your company, products, and services as they can on their own, and they want to remain anonymous as long as possible. The truth is, buyers want to be in control of *everything*, not just the research part of making a purchasing decision. And more than anything else, they want to be in control of how and when they are contacted.

Prospects aren't interested in hearing from you directly until they know you can help them and they are ready to receive your help. This can prove to be a challenge, especially when we want to control the marketing and sales process every step of the way.

Think of yourself when you are considering buying something. Do you want to be bombarded by phone calls, emails, and text messages while you are doing your initial research? Do you want to enter your email and/or phone number in an opt-in form just to get information that you need as part of your research? No, you don't. This brings us to Revenue Zone rule #2.

> **RULE**
> **#2**
> **Make it easy for your prospect to remain anonymous as long as they desire while doing their research and due diligence.**

We will discuss exactly how to accomplish this in upcoming chapters. For now, make sure that any marketing content or product/service information you have is easy to locate on your website and available without an opt-in. Also make sure that it is easy to find and access in other online locations where your prospect may be researching.

Again, we will explore all of this in much more detail later in this book.

THE B2B BUYING BEHAVIOR RULE

Early in my career, as I was transitioning from working as a software engineer into more of a sales and marketing role, I received some great advice from the top revenue producer in our company, and I have never forgotten it. She told me, "Tom, always remember, people love to buy but they hate to be sold."

This adage is now truer than ever. Not only do people not want to be sold, but they also want to be in control of their buying process. As I mentioned in Chapter 1, your B2B prospects want to buy the same way they do as consumers. They want to do their own research, come to their own decisions, and then purchase. They want to control the journey and talk with someone only when they are ready and only when that conversation is going to be consultative and valuable. Essentially, they want to be their own salesperson.

In many B2B purchases, there is a team or group making

a buying decision instead of an individual. In this case, the team or group still wants to feel in control of their buying process in the same way that they individually do as consumers. This brings us to Revenue Zone Rule #3.

> **RULE**
> **#3**
>
> **Help your prospects and customers control their Buyer's Journey by making it easy for them to get the information they need at the right time and in the right place.**

Offer your B2B prospects the information they need in a way that is easy to access and understand. Consider creating a Resource Center on your website that contains the most useful and relevant information your prospects are likely to look for at different stages in their journey. The bottom line is that you want to make it easy for your prospect to buy without ever feeling like they are being sold. We will delve into exactly how to do this in Chapter 5 as part of building your Yellow Brick Road.

A SHIFTING LANDSCAPE REQUIRES A SHIFT IN MINDSET

I have talked with many sales and marketing professionals who truly believe it is just a matter of time before the perfect disruptive storm somehow disappears and everything returns to "how it used to be."

However, as you review the three Revenue Zone rules in more detail, you will start to see that there is a mindset shift needed across the board in how we look at and go about sales and marketing. We all have to get it through our heads that *things are not going back to the way they used to be.*

That said, I completely understand that change can be difficult—particularly when you have built a successful career around doing things a certain way. The anxiety I experienced in my meeting revolved around the stark realization that I needed a major shift in my mindset and approach, and at the time, I had no idea how this would happen.

Take a minute and ask yourself the questions below. If your answers to the questions in the old-school section are "yes," consider how you can shift toward the Revenue Zone mindset and approach.

Old-School Mindset and Approach

- Am I trying to *insert myself* into my prospects' buyer's journey on my schedule and timeline?

- Am I trying to *convince* my prospect to make a purchase?

- Am I trying to *control* the sales process and buyer's journey?

Revenue-Zone Mindset and Approach

- Am I trying to get *invited* into my prospect's buyer's journey based on their needs, schedule, and timeline?

- Am I being a *valuable guide or a consultant* to my prospect?

- Am I *enabling* my prospect to effectively control their sales process and buyer's journey?

Now let's look at a real-world example of the three Revenue Zone rules and corresponding mindset shift in action.

LET'S BUY A CAR!

While not a B2B example, I want to take you through an example that you have most likely experienced and can relate to: buying a new car.

The Old-School Buying Experience

Recently, my friend Noelle was telling me about her experience at a local car dealership. She was looking to trade in her older, used car for a newer, used car. After carefully looking at her budget, she knew exactly how much she could afford for her monthly payment and what she was looking for in a "new" vehicle.

After doing her homework, Noelle went to the local dealership and was immediately approached by a salesperson. Noelle explained that she could afford $400 a month before taxes and insurance, that she wanted a car that was no more than five years old, and that good gas mileage was a priority.

"Well, that's a really specific list you have," the salesperson said.

"I wanted to make sure I came in prepared," Noelle said.

"I can see that," the salesperson said. "Let me see what we have that fits your list."

Noelle waited as the salesperson reviewed the options on his computer.

"It seems like we only have three cars on the lot that meet your specifications," the salesperson said.

"Great, can you print out the info for each one?" Noelle asked.

"Let me show you the cars first. They have information listed on the printouts in their windows," the salesperson said.

"What about a list of previous owners and service done to the car?" Noelle asked. "Do you have that as well?"

"Um, no. But you can pay to look it up yourself if you find a car you like."

Noelle silently followed the salesperson out to the lot.

"This one is great," the salesperson said. "Good gas mileage, and only seven years old."

"I thought I said I wanted something that wasn't any older than five years," Noelle said.

"Well, we don't have anything like that in your price range."

"You said there were three cars here that fit my requirements," Noelle said, sighing and running her hand through her hair.

"I had to be creative. We have this one, which fits your payment price. We also have two others that are newer, but a bit over your price-point," the salesperson said.

"So, you don't have any cars that match my list?" Noelle asked.

"Not here, no."

"Did you search at any of your other locations? Maybe we could have a car shipped here," Noelle suggested, trying to give the salesperson the benefit of the doubt.

"You don't want to go through all that, do you, when we have options here that are close to your needs?" the salesperson protested. "Let's do a test drive, and I am sure you will like one of the options we have here."

Can you guess what Noelle did? You're right! She left without buying, went home, and continued her search. Fortunately for Noelle, another dealer in town was more aligned with the Revenue Zone mindset.

The Revenue Zone Buying Experience

Noelle went back to her computer and found a car at a different dealership that matched her exact needs and criteria. The dealer's website allowed her to access a full history of the vehicle, included a payment calculator that provided payment options, and offered a phone-based consultation to walk through the payment terms and answer any questions.

Initially, Noelle was nervous about doing the consultation, as she expected that it would turn into a high-pressure sales pitch, but was pleasantly surprised when the salesperson simply walked her through the numbers in plain English and competently answered all her questions. He then said to schedule a time on his online calendar when she was ready to see the car or do a test drive, and he would make sure the car was ready to go when she arrived.

Noelle scheduled the test drive and went to the dealership. She was still a bit concerned that she might have a similar experience to the one she had at the other dealership—that they would try to convince her to buy something other than the particular car she wanted to look at.

However, once again, Noelle was pleasantly surprised when the salesperson had the exact car all ready for her, walked her through everything, and helped her with a test drive. I remember Noelle saying to me later, "He acted more like a consultant than a salesperson."

Noelle completed the test drive and bought the car. The paperwork was easy and straightforward, and not once did the salesperson try to pressure her or get her to consider another vehicle. Since then, Noelle has constantly talked about her great experience with this dealership with her friends and family. Guess where they are going next to buy a car?

THE DIFFERENCE

In Noelle's first dealership experience, the salesperson wanted to control the process and control what information Noelle had access to. The salesperson and dealership violated all three Revenue Zone rules and were certainly operating under an old-school mindset.

In her second experience, the dealership's website openly provided the information Noelle needed to do her research and due diligence. The salesperson acted as a trusted guide and consultant and embraced virtual business. He didn't try to change her experience, he facilitated it. Noelle was able to be in control of her own buyer's journey and was excited to make the purchase when she was ready.

Now, whenever Noelle hears that someone is in the market for a new car, she recommends the second dealership. She tells them about how amazing her experience was and that she is super happy with her car. She started out as a prospect but ended up as a salesperson and ambassador for the dealership.

This is the power that creating a well-cultivated, buyer-lead journey can have in your business. When you give people access to the information they need in an easy-to-understand format without trying to control what they do, you turn prospects into customers and customers into ambassadors for your brand.

B2B DIFFERENCES

Noelle's car purchase was a very important and significant buying decision for her. However, in Noelle's case, she did all the research and made the buying decision on her own.

In the B2B arena, most buying decisions are not made by a single person. More likely, there is a team or a larger group of stakeholders driving the buying process.

B2B teams also want to buy like they do as consumers. They want to do their own research, they only want to talk with salespeople when they are ready, they want guidance and consultation rather than being pressured, and they want to be in control of the buying process.

Of course, this can definitely make the overall sales and marketing process more complex and difficult than it would be if you were just dealing with a single buyer.

However, knowing and applying the Revenue Zone rules is even more essential when a group or team is making the buying decision and, when applied correctly, will give you and your company a major advantage over your competitors that are still operating with an old-school mindset.

In the upcoming chapters of this book, I am going to introduce principles, techniques, and strategies that can be utilized to get B2B teams—and individual buyers—into the Revenue Zone as quickly and efficiently as possible.

BE THE BUYER!

One of my all-time favorite movies is *Caddyshack*. In that movie, Ty Webb, played by Chevy Chase, tells Danny Noonan to "be the ball." The premise is that if he can "be the golf ball," he will become a much better golfer.

As we shift from the old-school mindset to the Revenue Zone mindset, it is important to put ourselves in the shoes of our prospects and customers and "be the buyer."

Answering the following questions related to your prospects and customers will enable you to better "be the buyer" and will increase the value you get from the Revenue Zone strategies and techniques laid out in the rest of this book.

- What is my buyer trying to accomplish?

- What problems is my buyer trying to solve?

- How can my product/service help my buyer solve their problems?

- What pain are these problems causing my buyer?

- Does my buyer consider my product/service a solution to their problems?

- How does my buyer view my product/service as different from competing options?

- What type of guidance and support would my buyer consider valuable during their buyer's journey?

- How can I enable my buyer to get all the relevant information they need while remaining anonymous and having their privacy respected?

Okay, let's move on now and look at how you can get your buyer successfully into the Revenue Zone.

Chapter Summary

- In order to navigate and weather the perfect disruptive storm, you need specific guidelines and rules to follow.

- The Revenue Zone has three rules that will guide you to success.

- Rule #1 - Become a valued consultant and guide for your prospects and customers.

- Rule #2 – Make it easy for your prospect to remain anonymous as long as they desire while doing their research and due diligence.

- Rule #3 – Help your prospects and customers control their buyer's journey by making it easy for them to get the information they need at the right time and in the right place.

- In addition to the three rules, it is important to shift from the old-school sales and marketing mindset to the Revenue Zone mindset.

- Noelle's car buying experience spotlights the difference between an old-school mindset and the Revenue Zone mindset.

- Noelle's experience can be applied to a B2B buyer journey that is driven by a team versus an individual. Recognize and accommodate the fact that teams still want to maintain control of their buying decisions.

- Instead of asking what *you* are trying to accomplish as a seller, ask what *your prospect* needs to become a buyer and accommodate their needs. Be the buyer!

- Recognize that when you facilitate a good buyer-controlled journey, you can turn your prospects into high-performing ambassadors for your company to their friends, family, and colleagues.

Discussion Questions

- How can you apply the three Revenue Zone rules in your business?

- How can you adjust to the Revenue Zone mindset and be more successful with your prospects and customers?

- How can you relate Noelle's car buying experience to your own business?

- How can you turn your prospects and customers into a high-performing sales team?

- How can you better "be the buyer"?

CHAPTER THREE

THE REVENUE ZONE MATRIX

Over my thirty-plus-year career, I have developed and implemented many marketing and sales funnels for my own businesses and for my clients. I love designing, creating, and implementing both B2B and B2C funnels, analyzing their performance, and then optimizing to continually improve their results.

In fact, one of the main reasons I created my digital marketing agency back in 2012 was that I wanted to design and build highly optimized funnels for my business clients. What I'm trying to convince you of here is that I have been a big fan of funnels my whole career, which makes what I am about to say next very difficult...

Traditional sales and marketing funnels are obsolete.

Okay, I said it! But before I continue, let me take a second and explain what I mean by "traditional sales and marketing funnels."

A traditional sales and marketing funnel revolves around using marketing and lead generation efforts to drive potential prospects into a tightly controlled sales process.

As prospects move through the funnel, many become disqualified (or they disqualify themselves), until the few remaining prospects at the end of the

The Traditional Sales and Marketing Funnel

funnel ultimately become customers. Of course, the goal of a good funnel is to keep as many prospects in the funnel for as long as possible by controlling the buyer journey as tightly as possible.

However, as we discussed in the last chapter, this is the

exact opposite of how prospects want to operate in today's world. Today, prospects want to control their own buyer's journey. Traditional funnels are designed to give prospects as little control as possible.

This is why marketing and salespeople everywhere need to pivot and adopt a more modern approach: the traditional funnel is no longer a workable model because it's all about controlling the buyer's journey. We must instead be willing to provide guidance to prospects and help facilitate their buyer's journey rather than trying to control it.

So, what is this more modern approach?

THE REVENUE ZONE MATRIX

The Revenue Zone Matrix ("RZ Matrix") is a system designed to move as many prospects as possible into the upper-right corner of the RZ Matrix to a place called the Revenue Zone.

Let's take a minute and revisit what the Revenue Zone is and what it isn't.

The Goal of the RZ Matrix

The Revenue Zone is a place in the buyer's journey where a prospect is **seriously considering spending money with your company for your products or services.**

This does not mean there is no other competition, and it does not mean the prospect is not seriously considering buying from others. It does not even mean they are "ready" to close and make the purchase.

What it does mean is that they are at a place where they are seriously considering doing business with your company.

When I use the term "prospect," I mean the company that is considering buying from you. In the B2B world, the prospect will likely consist of a group of people who contribute to the purchase decision, so for our purposes, we will assume the prospect represents a company and not a specific person. In the B2C world, of course, the prospect would most often be an individual.

For a prospect to enter the Revenue Zone, two things must be true:

1. **The prospect has a fairly high level of demand (a pressing need and excitement) for your product or service, and**

2. **The prospect has a reasonable level of trust and confidence in your company.**

These two requirements form the framework of the RZ Matrix.

The RZ Matrix, like all matrices, can be displayed by points and on a graph delineating different areas. But instead of using pairs of numbers to plot the points, we are going to use three specific stages on each axis to measure and monitor the ascension of the prospect into the Revenue Zone.

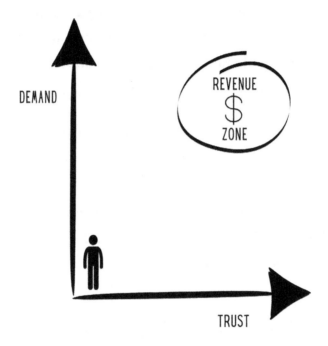

The Revenue Zone Criteria

On the vertical axis, we measure whether the prospect has **awareness of**, **interest in**, or **demand for** your product or service. On the horizontal axis, we measure the quality and relevance of the relationship that exists between the prospect and your company by marking whether they **know you**, **like you**, or **trust you**.

The Demand Axis (Vertical)

Awareness: The entry-point on the vertical axis of the RZ Matrix is *awareness,* which simply means that the prospect has some level of awareness of your product or service. They could have only a tiny amount of awareness, but a prospect can only be on the RZ Matrix if they have at least some level of awareness of what you do. No business will buy from you if they have no idea what you sell, so it doesn't make sense to call them a prospect until they do.

Interest: The next level up is *interest.* This means that not only is the prospect aware of your existence, but they also have some level of interest in how your products or services can help them solve a problem, address a pain point, or provide other value in their business. In this stage, prospects are likely conducting research and working to better understand your products or services.

Demand: Have you ever wanted something really badly? Maybe a new car, a new bicycle, or a new computer? If so, you can probably recall experiencing an emotional feeling—combined with logical reasoning—pushing you toward that thing that you really wanted. This state is what I refer to as *demand,* and as far as prospects' ascension up this vertical axis goes, our ultimate goal is to get them to this state. When prospects demand what you offer, prospects have a real need for what you offer and a clear understanding of how your products or services will benefit their business.

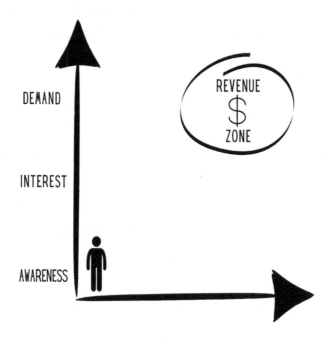

The Y Axis

Now, of course, the prospect's ascension is a continuum rather than an absolute. Prospects' demand can fluctuate, with their demand growing stronger or weaker from day to day. In any case, a prospect will always enter your

RZ Matrix with low awareness and, hopefully, ascend to higher levels of awareness into *interest* and, ultimately, to *demand*.

However, demand alone does not put a prospect in the Revenue Zone. The other half of the equation relates to the relationship the prospect has developed with you, your business, your team, and potentially even with your customers (or other prospects).

The Trust Axis (Horizontal)

Know: Just like awareness on the vertical axis, this first stage is where your prospect enters your RZ matrix on the horizontal axis. *Know* means that the prospect has some knowledge that you or your company exist (this is different from being aware that your *product* or *service* exists). Maybe they know some of your team members from a trade show or from social media. However the connection came about, they have some knowledge of your company or its people.

Like: The next stage on the trust scale is *like*. What this means is that the prospect is experiencing some level of affinity for you, your team, or your company.

It is important to note that this affinity does not have to come about from personal conversations or one-on-one interactions. Rather, this affinity will more likely come about based on what the prospect learns about you and your company as they do their research and their overall experience with your company. You can also win points in your prospects' eyes by making their research easy for them. Remember Noelle's car shopping experience? Which dealer did Noelle end up liking best? This affinity is not just because you are "nice" or easy to work with (though those could contribute); it mainly comes from the relevance, assistance, and value you provide to the prospect as they progress in their buyer's journey.

Trust: As you continue to add more and more value (in a friendly and professional manner), the prospect will ultimately begin to *trust* you and your company. They will become convinced that you can truly help them solve their problem or achieve their target outcome now and in the future. This trust level is based on the authenticity, knowledge, and value they receive from you and your company. They want to know you're honest, that you have the experience to help them, and that you can get them real results based on the value you and your company bring to the relationship.

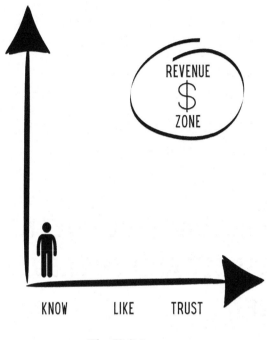

The X Axis

In summary, in order to get your prospects to ascend into the Revenue Zone, you must do two things:

1. Move prospects up the vertical axis in terms of their *awareness*, *interest*, and *demand* for your products or services.

> **2.** Move prospects to the right on the horizontal axis by helping them *know*, *like*, and *trust* your business, your brand, and your team.

Unfortunately, this is not as easy and straightforward in application as it may seem.

WHAT STANDS BETWEEN THE PROSPECT AND THE REVENUE ZONE?

The question is now this: How do you get a prospect from the bottom left corner of the RZ Matrix into the Revenue Zone? And, more importantly, how do you do this repeatedly, predictably, and consistently?

In Chapter 2 we discussed how prospects want to be in control of the buying process and how they will, in most cases, work to remain anonymous as long as possible as they do their own research. But *why* do they want to remain anonymous?

You guessed it! They do not want to be nagged or pressured by a salesperson, especially when they're really just trying to learn more about your product(s) or service(s) and your company.

The fact is that we, as sales and marketing professionals, have driven our prospects undercover through aggressive sales follow-ups, spam emails, and other intrusive marketing actions. Because of this, prospects have developed consistent behavior for each point of the matrix to ward off old-school, high-pressure sales tactics.

So, like it or not, we have to accept and adapt to the fact that most prospects are going to start out (and potentially spend a fair amount of time) in what I call "the Anonymous Zone" when they first enter the RZ Matrix.

THE ANONYMOUS ZONE

Inside this area of the RZ Matrix, the prospect is researching your products or services to learn more about your company, your brand reputation, and the unique value your products or services offer—all while trying to stay as incognito as possible. They visit your website and your social media channels, check your Google reviews, sort through other online resources, and talk to colleagues.

While researching you, the prospect is also probably taking the same steps to check out your competitors. The main reason that prospects try to stay in the Anonymous Zone is that they do not want to be interrupted, disrupted, or pressured into making a decision.

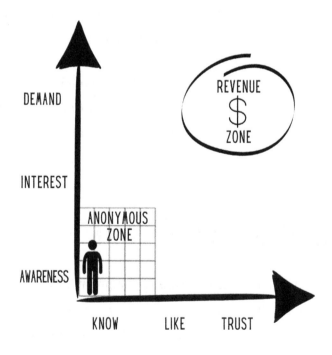

The Anonymous Zone

Right now, you are probably wondering how you can guide a prospect in the Anonymous Zone. That is a good question, and I will address it in detail in Chapters 4 and 5. For now, it is important to understand that the Anonymous Zone exists and is a critical stage of the RZ Matrix.

ARE PROSPECTS REALLY MORE INFORMED THAN EVER?

With all the advances we've seen in online data and information sharing, many marketers and sales professionals conclude that the average prospect is "more informed than ever." However, based on my research and my experience working with prospects, I have found that statement to be false.

Yes, prospects certainly have more data and information than ever. But this abundance of data frequently results in information overload. It's also easy for prospects to get confused as they try to sort through conflicting opinions, ratings, and advice.

As a result, prospects can feel overwhelmed. This feeling results in an overall lack of clarity and, worse yet, distrust and indecision. Feeling overwhelmed also causes prospects to either get stuck in the Anonymous Zone or to jump out of the RZ Matrix altogether.

The Engagement Zone

The remaining zone in the RZ Matrix is the Engagement Zone—the area that lies between the Anonymous Zone and the Revenue Zone.

The Engagement Zone represents the point where prospects are willing to identify themselves and possibly even have a conversation with someone in your business. This willingness may come about due to a need to see a demo or sample of your product or to get answers to more detailed questions than are addressed online. In many cases, prospects reach out simply to validate that the information they discovered online is valid and up to date.

The bottom line is these prospects are now willing to engage with your business and the sales team—which is great news! But be careful: many sales teams mistake the Engagement Zone for the Revenue Zone.

Misclassifying a prospect's zone can result in the prospect

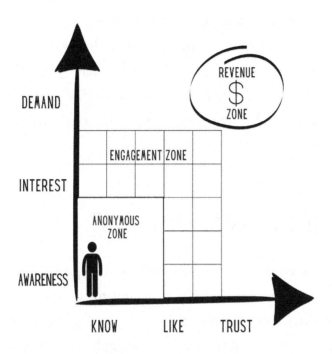

The Engagement Zone

moving the prospect backward in the RZ Matrix and possibly out of it altogether. You must realize that a willingness to engage does not mean the prospect is seriously considering spending money with your business (at least not yet…).

You should also note that the Engagement Zone may not exist for your business or many of your prospects may desire an "engagement free" experience. Depending on your industry and the products or services you are selling, your prospects may stay in the Anonymous Zone all the way up the RZ Matrix until they reach the Revenue Zone. However, if you successfully implement your Yellow Brick Road as outlined in Chapters 4 and 5 your prospects will be excited to enter (and use to their advantage) the Engagement Zone.

WHAT ABOUT OPT-INS?

Another common misconception is that prospects enter the Engagement Zone when they "opt-in" on your website or landing page in order to access gated content. Unfortunately, this is rarely the case. Usually, they are in the Anonymous Zone, researching and gathering information. This is why you will often get spam addresses or other bogus information from your opt-in forms.

I am not a big fan of gated content in the Anonymous Zone because is it violates Revenue Zone Rule #2 (make it easy for your prospect to remain anonymous while they research). In addition, the Privacy Paradigm is continually making getting valid email addresses more and more challenging.

Rather, I have discovered that if you easily provide the

content a prospect is looking for with little or no friction, they will legitimately end up in the Revenue Zone faster and be ready to actively engage as much as needed to get there.

FROM THE REVENUE ZONE TO REVENUE

Before we continue, I want to spotlight a couple more points related to the Revenue Zone. Just because a prospect is in the Revenue Zone doesn't mean they are ready to buy or make a purchase. While prospects are "seriously considering spending money with your business," when in the Revenue Zone, there is still work to be done to transition those prospects into paying customers.

There are two more qualification points that prospects in the Revenue Zone need to hit for them to be ready to purchase. You can assess their readiness with two questions:

1. **Do they have the available budget to make the purchase?**

2. Do they have an "impending event"?

What I mean by "available budget" is pretty straight-forward. Answering "yes" to that question means your prospects have enough dollars earmarked to make the purchase. In B2B sales, this often requires approval from someone beyond the primary person making the purchase decision.

By "impending event," I mean that there is some future event that is literally going to force a decision to be made and cause the prospect to commit and purchase. This could be an internal deadline, an external mandate, an upcoming board meeting, a budget that needs to be utilized before the end of a fiscal year, or anything else. It does not matter what it is, but it is important to know that, in B2B sales, impending events are what drive decisions (and purchases).

Many sales teams try to create impending events with end-of-month or end-of-quarter discounts and other incentives. Sometimes these offers are sufficiently motivating to function as valid impending events. But if you understand

and appreciate your prospect's true impending event, you will have a far better chance of converting them into a paying customer. You'll also do so with fewer discounts and less stress.

Understanding the prospect's impending event allows you to better guide and support them in the final steps of making the decision to purchase your product or service.

The fastest and easiest way to transition a prospect in the Revenue Zone into a paying customer is to make sure the prospect has the necessary budget and a clearly defined impending event.

DEFINING *YOUR* REVENUE ZONE

Remember, the Revenue Zone is a place in the buyer's journey where your prospect is seriously considering spending money with your company for your products or services.

But how does this relate to your specific RZ Matrix? What does *your* Revenue Zone look like? How do you apply this to your specific products or services?

Excellent questions! Let's take a minute and see how you can adapt the definition of the Revenue Zone to your business.

First off, you need to work out which product or service you are building your RZ Matrix to support. For companies that have just one product or service (or one general category of products or services), this will be very straightforward.

However, if your company has multiple, unrelated products or services (or categories of products or services), then you will likely need to build out multiple RZ Matrices for your business. For now, select just one product or service that you want to focus on.

Next, work out what the prospect needs to *understand* and *believe* about your product or service and your company for them to be in the Revenue Zone.

For example, let's say your company sells accounting software to small business owners. What would your prospect (in this case a small business owner) need to understand and believe about your software and company to be seriously considering spending money with your business?

They would need to **understand** the following:

- **How your software will benefit their business.**

- **That your software is affordable and easy to use.**

- **How your company will help them successfully implement and use the software.**

In addition, here is what they would need to **believe**:

- **That your accounting software is a better choice than competing options available.**

- **That you are a great company to work with and that you have their best interest in mind.**

- **That they need to take action now and get your software deployed in their business as soon as possible.**

If a prospect has these understandings and beliefs, they are most likely in the Revenue Zone and seriously considering spending money with your company.

Your task is to repeat this same exercise for your product

or service. Identify three understandings and three beliefs that need to be in place for your prospect to be in the Revenue Zone. Please keep it simple: three points each are plenty for this exercise.

Once you have worked out your key understandings and beliefs, make sure they align with the axes of your RZ Matrix. Verify that there is clear *demand* and *trust* present in these understandings and beliefs.

Thinking about your current customers can help you identify the buying mindset for your product or service. Ask yourself what the people who buy from you *understand* and *believe* about your company and offer. Use your answers to refine your points.

Once you feel comfortable with your three understandings and three beliefs, write them down and put them in a safe place. We will be using this later in Chapter 5.

Congratulations! You have now defined your Revenue Zone for a specific product or service. This will be super important in upcoming chapters as we work out your Yellow Brick Road and facilitate prospects reaching your Revenue Zone in large numbers.

THE GENESIS OF THE REVENUE ZONE MATRIX

Before we leave this chapter, I want to take a minute and talk more about the genesis of the RZ Matrix.

While I don't really like to use the word "revolutionary," I honestly believe the RZ Matrix and the related techniques we are going to cover in the remainder of this book are, in fact, revolutionary.

The RZ Matrix was inspired by that moment when I lost confidence in my sales presentation and the rationale behind it. At that moment, I certainly did not know what the exact solution was, but I knew that something was broken and needed to be fixed.

The RZ Matrix as presented here evolved from the research, discovery, and testing I was doing long before the day of my infamous presentation. But until that day, I was not totally convinced (or maybe was not ready to be convinced) that I needed to completely switch my mindset and take a new viewpoint on the buyer's journey, traditional sales and marketing, and the principles underlying the RZ Matrix.

In Chapters 4 and 5, I will give you a proven strategy—a system called "the Yellow Brick Road"—that will facilitate your prospects moving from the lower-left corner of the RZ Matrix into the Revenue Zone without any high-control, high-pressure sales tactics.

Let the journey continue!

Chapter Summary

- Traditional sales and marketing funnels have become obsolete as prospects want buyer-controlled journeys that allow them to be in control of their sales process.

- The RZ Matrix is a new and modern alternative to traditional funnels.

- The RZ Matrix is composed of two axes, each of which has three stages.

- The vertical axis ascends from *awareness* to *interest* to *demand*.

- The horizontal axis progresses from *know* to *like* to *trust*.

- Inside the RZ matrix, there are three areas: the Anonymous Zone, the Engagement Zone, and the Revenue Zone.

- Prospects will pass through two zones on the road to the Revenue Zone: the Anonymous Zone and (potentially) the Engagement Zone.

- Prospects are not necessarily more informed than

ever, but they do have an overwhelming amount of information and data available to them.

- Once a prospect reaches the Revenue Zone, they must have two things to become a customer: a budget and an impending event.

- The Revenue Zone for your specific product or service is formed when you identify three understandings and three beliefs that your prospect must have to seriously consider buying from your business.

- The genesis of the RZ Matrix goes back long before my transformational sales presentation but has evolved rapidly as a result of that event.

Discussion Questions

- Why is the RZ Matrix more applicable in today's world than a traditional sales and marketing funnel?

- How do you like to buy? Do you like to be in control of your own research and buyer's journey? How and when do you want to engage with a salesperson?

- How do the different RZ Matrix stages (along the axes) apply to your business?

- How do the different RZ Matrix zones apply to your business?

- How can you identify an impending event that will move your prospects from the Revenue Zone to revenue?

CHAPTER FOUR

YOUR YELLOW BRICK ROAD

"Yellow Brick Road (n):
The road to success or happiness…"
~ Collins English Dictionary

We live in California now, but my wife grew up in Portsmouth, New Hampshire and still has a lot of family in the Portsmouth area. We try to go back and visit a couple of times each year, and on one of our trips a few years back, my wife suggested that we stay in Boston for a few days and visit the Museum of Fine Arts.

Now, I am not a big art person and honestly was not thrilled by the idea of spending the better part of the day roaming around a museum looking at art collections that I knew very little about.

However, I agreed to go, and we arrived at the museum bright and early to get our tickets. As we were paying our admission, they asked if we wanted to purchase a self-guided audio tour that would guide us through the various exhibits and provide details about the collections in each one. (I believe they have a mobile app for this now, but you had to purchase their device and headphones at the time.)

The program gave us the option to go on various tours based on which exhibits we wanted to see or to just move around the museum on our own and get details about the individual paintings by entering the number of the specific exhibit we were viewing.

It sounded like a great idea, so we purchased the self-guided audio tour and started our journey.

A quick aside: There I was in a very large museum. I was *aware* that the museum contained art exhibits, and I *knew* I was in the Boston Museum of Fine Arts. So I was essentially sitting in the bottom left corner of the RZ Matrix for this experience.

Okay, let's continue. We selected a suggested route provided in the audio tour and began moving from gallery to gallery in the recommended sequence. I soon found myself more and more *interested* in the art in each gallery and the history behind the collections, and I was starting to really *like* the museum and the experience they were providing.

By the end of the day, my wife and I had visited many of the exhibitions, collections, and galleries based on the guidance of the audio tour. We both had very tired feet, but it ended up being a great experience, and the guided tour sparked my interest in art and art history.

Now, I can't say I was in the Revenue Zone because I was not quite ready to run out and buy any expensive paintings, but I definitely ascended in the RZ Matrix and became a big fan of the Boston Museum of Fine Arts.

So, how did this happen? Through the audio tour, the museum successfully guided and facilitated our journey. They did not force the journey; instead, they provided recommendations and direction on how we could move through the museum.

Furthermore, they also enlightened and educated us at every stage and made it easy for us to move forward. The bottom line is that they had created a Yellow Brick Road, and we successfully followed it.

YOUR YELLOW BRICK ROAD

So how do you use the RZ Matrix to actually get prospects into the Revenue Zone predictably and at a rapid pace? And how do you do this, knowing prospects want to stay anonymous for as long as possible, be in control of their own buyer's journey, and are likely to be overwhelmed if there is too much disparate information and data from many different sources?

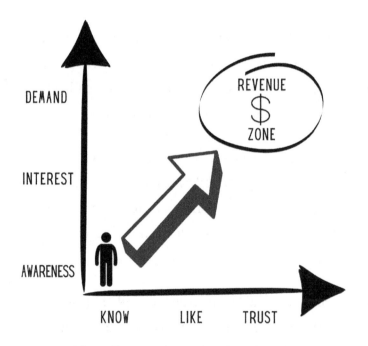

The Yellow Brick Road to the Revenue Zone

The secret here is providing your prospects with a roadmap, just like the one my wife and I received at the museum.

You need to provide your prospects a guide that will help them navigate through your RZ Matrix while providing maximum value to them, creating little or no friction, and minimizing their chance of information overload.

This road map is what I call your "Yellow Brick Road (YBR)." The Yellow Brick Road commences when the prospect first enters your RZ Matrix and represents the most successful "route" that a typical prospect would follow to reach the Revenue Zone in the shortest amount of time.

Try to recall a time when you were a prospect researching a product or service that you were interested in. Was it easy to find all the information you were looking for, or did you feel like you were cutting your way through a jungle of information and falling down rabbit holes?

Surely it would have been better if someone had cleared a path for you—or perhaps they successfully did—that you could navigate without risk of spiky branches or dangling poisonous snakes?

The best way to encourage a prospect to move through your RZ Matrix is to make sure they have an easy-to-travel path.

If you do not have a clearly defined and well-mapped YBR, the probability of your prospect reaching the Revenue Zone is not very high, and they will more than likely drop out of your RZ Matrix, never to be seen again.

The process of building your YBR can take a bit of work, and you may need to involve different people from different parts of your business in the process. However, this work will pay big dividends, and you will have a huge competitive advantage over your competitors who do not have their YBR defined and implemented.

The job of the YBR is to keep prospects who have entered your RZ Matrix moving forward in their journey along both axes, while at the same time removing doubts, objections, and barriers along the way in a manner that facilitates and guides (but does not force) their journey to becoming a paying customer.

As we know, the prospect wants to be in control of their research and buying process. They want to make their own decisions, and they generally don't want to talk with salespeople. Instead, they want to remain in the Anonymous Zone as long as they possibly can.

We also have to recognize that traveling the YBR is a journey, not an event, and that the journey will be supported by many more "bricks"—or touch points—along the way to the Revenue Zone.

In the remainder of this chapter, I am going to help you work out what bricks you have available in your brickyard (you probably have a lot more than you think) and get them identified and categorized. You will also be introduced to a free online tool that will help you with this process (and future steps).

Then, in the next chapter, I will walk you through the process of actually constructing your YBR using the bricks that you have curated from your brickyard.

DO YOU KNOW WHAT IS IN YOUR BRICKYARD?

The prospect's journey along your YBR will be influenced, and to a large degree guided, by five key areas (not necessarily in this order):

1. Your online presence

2. Your content

3. Your product and service offerings

4. Your customers, partners, and influencers

5. Your internal team

These five areas contain the specific bricks that you have available for building a YBR that will facilitate a smooth, buyer-controlled journey. Let's examine each of these areas in more detail.

#1 - YOUR COMPANY'S ONLINE PRESENCE

"Online presence" refers to how your company and your products or services are portrayed and represented online. Your online presence can be broken down into four categories:

- **Your Website** - This includes everything on your website, including your Home page, About Us page, Contact page, and any pages that make up your website.

- **Branded Search** - Branded search refers to what is displayed when someone searches for your company name or your product or service brands on Google, YouTube (which is the world's second-largest search engine behind Google), or any other search engine.

- **Social Media** – This includes everything that is available on any of your social media properties such as LinkedIn, Twitter, Facebook, etc., and includes posts and any comments or other public conversations.

- **Review Sites** - This includes any third-party review site covering your industry where companies or products are rated or discussed.

#2 - YOUR CONTENT

By content, I mean any strictly informational content that your company has created and published either on your website, social media, blog, videos on YouTube, etc. Content can generally be broken down into three categories:

- **Educational** - This can be any content that is designed to educate your prospect on a topic related to the problems your company is working to solve, implementing or utilizing your products or services, the market you are serving, etc. It also includes any specific case studies you have on your customers using your product or service in their business.

- **Thought Leadership** - Thought leadership content differs from educational content in that it is more editorial or opinionated in nature and less tutorialistic. An example of thought leadership content could be a blog post on the state of your industry or a video on market trends that could impact your prospects and customers.

- **Marketing** - Marketing content is content directly related to the features, functionality, and value proposition of your products or services. This could include brochures, pricing information on your website, a product demo, or even a proposal, estimate, or quote that is provided to a prospect.

Content can be published in many different formats (including video) both online and offline. For our purposes, the content we are referring to here is created internally within your company and not by partners or other external influencers (I will address partners and influencers later).

#3 - YOUR PRODUCT OR SERVICE OFFERINGS

Product and service offerings refer to what you are actually selling and the value it provides to your customers. By "offerings" I mean:

- Everything related to a product or service, including price and what is explicitly included or not included.

- Any post-sale support and training that you provide.

- Any trials, free versions, or samples of your products or services.

- Any bonuses or add-ons that could be included such as free shipping, etc.

- Any guarantees or risk reversal mechanisms that you offer.

- Anything else related to what your customers are purchasing from your business.

#4 - YOUR CUSTOMERS, PARTNERS, AND INFLUENCERS

Your customers, partners, and influencers are an external third-party "ecosystem" that can support, influence, or detract from your prospect reaching the Revenue Zone. This group includes:

- **Customers** - Current and past customers: everyone who has ever purchased from you.

- **Partners** - Other companies and individuals you work with that are marketing or selling your products or services, including resellers, distributors, sales agents, dealers, etc. It also includes agencies, consultants, and others who provide services on your behalf.

- **Influencers** - Influencers such as press, analysts, media, popular figures on social media, or any other third party that is not a partner or customer but that understands and has an opinion (good or bad) about your company, products, or services.

Before we continue, I want to take a minute and emphasize how important this area of customers, partners, and influencers will be to the success of your YBR.

As we discussed in earlier chapters, prospects do not respond to hype and outrageous claims. They want to make their buying decision based on their own research and due diligence. And they want to know what others have learned and discovered based on their research and experience with your company and your products and services.

The best way to get prospects to believe that you can really help them is to have other customers, partners, and influencers tell them. This can take the form of written testimonials, video case studies where your customer explains the benefits they received from your product or service, or success stories on social media platforms.

Word of mouth is one of the few old-school models in business that still consistently reaps big rewards. If a prominent customer, partner, or influencer is singing the praises to your company, product, or service, it will provide a huge tailwind to your YBR.

#5 - YOUR INTERNAL TEAM

Last—but certainly not least—is your internal team, which includes anyone who interacts in some capacity with your prospects and customers. Generally, however, your internal team can be broken down into four categories:

- **Sales and Marketing** - Anyone who is involved in generating new prospects or working with existing prospects.

- **Customer Support and Service** - Anyone who supports or assists existing customers.

- **Administration** - Your accounting, billing, legal, or other administrative staff.

- **Executives** - Your C-level executives or other members of your senior management team including founders and owners that may, when appropriate, interact with your prospects and customers.

The individual items within each of these five areas are what fill up your brickyard and from which you'll build out your Yellow Brick Road (as you will learn how to do in the next chapter). Now it is time to take inventory of your bricks. Fortunately, I have a special tool to help you accomplish this quickly and easily.

BRICKYARD INVENTORY

Now that you are familiar with the different areas that can influence your YBR, it is time to create an inventory and assessment of the potential bricks that you have available to construct your YBR. I will call this set of potential bricks your "brickyard."

As I mentioned, I have created a special online tool to help with this process. It's also completely free!

Depending on your company, the next few steps will likely require multiple members of your team working together. I recommend that someone in your organization acts as the primary leader and coordinator for this effort and that you work to have your brickyard identified and documented in three days or less.

Let's get started!

STEP #1 - VISIT THE REVENUE ZONE YELLOW BRICK ROAD RESOURCE CENTER

Go to therevenuezone.com/ybrbuilder and make a copy of the Yellow Brick Road Builder sheet for your own use. You can also view detailed instructional videos on how to use the Builder and check out some Yellow Brick Road examples. If you would like to be alerted of updates to the Builder or the Resource Center, you can enter your email to receive relevant updates. The tool is completely free.

STEP #2 - INVENTORY, CATEGORIZE, AND ASSESS

The next step in the process is to inventory, categorize, and assess the bricks that you have available to support the assembly of your Yellow Brick Road.

Open your copy of the Yellow Brick Road Builder sheet that you created in Step #1. The first tab in the Builder includes a copy of these same instructions for your convenience. Now open the second tab labeled "Online Presence."

The first section on this page is related to your website. I have listed the most common pages that exist on business websites in the Builder. If your site is organized differently, please make any updates needed based on the pages that exist on your website. If your website is large and has many pages, only select the top ten most relevant and commonly visited pages.

Now we are going to do a quick analysis and assessment of each website page you've listed. Using the drop down in each column, select how much or how little each page accomplishes the following:

1. **Create Demand** - Does this page move the prospect to greater levels of *demand* on the y-axis of the RZ Matrix? Options include "Yes," "Somewhat," "No," and "N/A."

2. **Build Trust** - Does this page move the prospect to higher levels of *trust* on the x-axis of the RZ Matrix? Options include "Yes," "Somewhat" "No" and "N/A."

3. **Potential Impact** - Overall, what potential impact does this page have on the prospect's Buyer's Journey and on their road to the Revenue Zone? Options include "Positive," "Neutral," "Negative," and "N/A."

Please do not over analyze or over think your assessment responses. Just make a quick evaluation for each page and select the appropriate option. Each time you make a selection from the dropdown, that cell will be automatically color coded based on your selection.

Online Presence	Creates Demand	Builds Trust	Potential Impact	Journey Sequence	Notes
Website					
Home Page	Yes	Somewhat	Positive		
About Us Page	Yes	Yes	Positive		
Contact Us Page	No	Somewhat	Neutral		
Pricing Page					
Product and Services Page					
Testimonials					
Blog					
Resources					
Other					
Branded Search					
Google Branded Search	Yes	Yes	Positive		
Bing Branded Search	Somewhat	Somewhat	Neutral		
YouTube Branded Search	No	No	Negative		
Social Media					
LinkedIn					

YBR Builder - The Online Presence Tab

Do not fill in anything at this point in the column labeled "Journey Sequence." This column will be used later in Chapter 5. However, feel free to make any notes or comments related to the page or your assessment rating in the "Notes" column.

Now continue with the next section labeled "Branded Search." Recall that a branded search refers to what is displayed when someone searches for your company name or your product or service brands on Google, YouTube or any other search engine.

Conduct a branded search of your company's name in Google, Bing, and YouTube and review the results. Using the same assessment options described previously, decide how your branded search results rank with respect to creating demand, building trust, and impacting the prospect's Buyer's Journey.

Next, address the sections on social media and review sites using the same process. Then move on and complete each section in the "Content," "Offerings," "Partners," "Influencers," and "Internal Team" tabs.

Do not do anything with the "My Revenue Zone" and "The Five Milestones" tabs at this point. These tabs will be used in the next chapter as you start to construct your YBR.

Note: many of the sections have space for up to ten items. You definitely do not need to list ten items for each section, and I highly recommend that you keep things simple by listing fewer items whenever possible.

Your goal here is to get a snapshot of what you have available to help guide your prospects and to assess the potential value and impact of each brick in your brickyard.

MISSING AND CRACKED BRICKS

As you work through the inventory, categorization, and assessment of your potential bricks, you will likely find that you have some missing bricks or possibly bricks that are "cracked" and, per your assessment, could have a negative impact on your prospects.

Do not worry about these missing or cracked bricks yet. I have found through experience that most companies have plenty of good bricks that can be used to construct an effective YBR today. Other bricks can be added and repaired over time. It is important to keep moving and not get bogged down. When you identify missing or cracked bricks, just make a note on your sheet and continue forward.

Once you have completed your inventory, categorization, and assessment, you are ready to move on to Chapter 5 and construct your Yellow Brick Road.

Onward!

Chapter Summary

- The purpose of your Yellow Brick Road (YBR) is to provide your prospects with a guided roadmap to the Revenue Zone.

- Your YBR, once created, will be a big competitive advantage for your company.

- The goal of the YBR is keeping your prospects engaged and progressing along both axes of the RZ Matrix.

- Your YBR will include "bricks" that represent potential touchpoints that can change prospects' perception of your company, product, or service.

- Bricks fit into five main areas:

  1. Your online presence

  2. Your content

  3. Your product and service offerings

  4. Your customers, partners, and influencers

  5. Your internal team

- Collectively, every position, asset, or item you currently have across these five areas comprise your brickyard.

- The bricks in your brickyard will be used to construct your YBR. The first step in the process is creating an inventory of what you have to work with, organized by each of the five areas.

- There is a free online tool called the YBR Builder that will help you with this process (therevenuezone. com/ybrbuilder).

- Your goal should be to complete the inventory and assessment process quickly—within three days or less.

- Once you have completed the inventory process and documented in the YBR Builder tool, you have defined your brickyard and are ready to move to the next chapter.

Discussion Questions

- How could a functional YBR be a big competitive advantage?

- How can the RZ Matrix and the YBR influence your overall marketing and sales processes?

- Is your company ready to build a YBR?

- Who in your company should be involved in defining your brickyard?

- How will you get this process done in three days or less?

CHAPTER FIVE

ONE BRICK AT A TIME: CONSTRUCTING YOUR YELLOW BRICK ROAD

YOUR PROVEN PROCESS

Early in my career, when I was transitioning from software engineering to the sales and marketing side of the business, I spent a lot of time observing and studying our sales team. I was fascinated by how some of our salespeople made the sales process look easy and always exceeded their goals, while others struggled and rarely achieved their quotas.

At first, I thought it was just personality or the education level of the salesperson. But as I observed more closely, I started to see a common theme develop with our most successful salespeople: *they had a proven process.*

What I mean by "proven process" is that these successful salespeople had a very specific sales process they followed with each of their prospects—and they did not vary from that process. For example, one salesperson refused to schedule a demonstration of our software with a prospect unless the prospect had carefully read a white paper about our software and provided a clear list of questions and requirements based on what they read. This was part of the exact sales process he followed, and he required his prospects to follow it as well.

On the other hand, our salespeople who were below-average performers rarely followed a proven or consistent process. They tended to *react* to each prospect and each situation versus following a clear process.

"Now wait a minute," you may wonder. "Doesn't the idea of a proven process violate everything I've learned so far about letting prospects control their Buyer's Journey with salespeople acting as guides and facilitators rather than trying to control the sales process?"

The answer is both "yes" and "no."

A proven roadmap is actually a very good thing for a prospect. It helps them get the information they need at the right time and in the right sequence. In my example above, the software demo was always much more valuable to the prospect when they had thoroughly read the white paper first and formulated a list of questions.

Think of the proven process as the roadmap that will help the prospect reach the Revenue Zone as efficiently as possible—or disqualify them if they are not really a good fit for your product or service. This is a good thing for both your company and your prospects.

The big difference between the Revenue-Zone mindset and the old-school mindset is that the prospect is driving the process and we are facilitating and guiding them on their journey. So rather than a salesperson insisting the prospect reads the white paper before scheduling a demo of the software, the Yellow Brick Road inherently guides the prospect in this direction as part of their journey.

Here is the best news: If your Yellow Brick Road is intelligently constructed, your prospects become their own salespeople and naturally move themselves through the proven process that is baked into your Yellow Brick Road. What a great way to make consistent sales and drive predictable revenue growth!

Your charter when constructing your Yellow Brick Road is to digitally emulate your proven process so that the prospect can get the right information, at the right time, and in the right sequence all on their own.

CONSTRUCTING YOUR YELLOW BRICK ROAD

At this point, you should have completed the inventory, categorization, and assessment of your bricks (using the Yellow Brick Road Builder tool). If you have, then you know what you have available in your brickyard. Well done!

Now let's work on constructing your YBR using these bricks. If you have not done so already, reopen your Yellow Brick Road Builder and go to the "My Revenue Zone" tab.

As you may recall, at the end of Chapter 3, you defined the Revenue Zone for your business by identifying three understandings and three beliefs that need to be in place for your prospect to be in the Revenue Zone. You then validated these key understandings and beliefs by ensuring that they aligned with the axes of your RZ Matrix and represented clear *demand* and *trust*.

In Chapter 3, I asked you to write down these key under-standings and beliefs and put them in a safe place. Now is the time to go back to that safe place, grab what you wrote, and add your three understandings and three beliefs into the "My Revenue Zone" tab in the Builder. Done? Excellent. Let's continue!

The 3 Understandings

How the software will benefit their business.

The software is affordable and easy to use.

How the company will help them successfully implement and use the software.

The 3 Beliefs

Our accounting software is a better choice than competing options available.

Our company will be great to work with and have their best interests in mind.

That it is important to take action now and get the software deployed in their business as soon as possible.

YBR Builder - My Revenue Zone Tab

THE FIVE MILESTONES

The next step in constructing your Yellow Brick Road is defining five key milestones that the prospect will pass through on their journey to the Revenue Zone.

The good news is that you have already defined your fifth milestone as this final milestone represents the goal of reaching the Revenue Zone.

Let's go back to the example of the small business accounting software company that we introduced in Chapter 3.

In this example, the three key **understandings** the prospect needed to have in order to be in the Revenue Zone were:

1. How the software will benefit their business.

2. That the software is affordable and easy to use.

3. How the company will help them successfully integrate and use the software.

And the three key **beliefs** were:

1. That the company's accounting software is a better

choice than competing options available.

2. The company will be great to work with and has their best interests in mind.

3. That they need to take action now and get the software deployed in their business as soon as possible.

When these three key understandings and beliefs are in place the prospect will have reached the Revenue Zone and achieved the fifth milestone.

However, when a prospect enters the Revenue Zone Matrix at the lower-left corner, none of these understandings or beliefs are in place. And not all these beliefs and understandings are going to be formulated at once. They are going to evolve and develop as the prospect ascends in the RZ Matrix.

The 5 Milestones to the Revenue Zone

As a result, we now want to identify four additional milestones that can be achieved along the way. For our purposes, **a milestone is simply an understanding or a belief that is reached along the prospect's journey.**

Once we have identified all of our milestones, we will select five bricks from our brickyard that will support each individual milestone being achieved. More on this in a minute.

In our example with the accounting software company, here are four milestones that a prospect would likely need to reach before they could ultimately ascend into the Revenue Zone (and achieve the fifth and final milestone).

- Milestone #1 - The prospect has a good understanding of the features and benefits of our accounting software.

- Milestone #2 - The prospect believes that these features and benefits will address their specific needs and requirements.

- Milestone #3 - The prospect understands how the software will be implemented and the cost and effort associated with the implementation.

- Milestone #4 - The prospect believes that this software and company is the best choice compared to other options on the market.

Now, these are just examples, and other relevant milestones could also be included. But when constructing your Yellow Brick Road, you want to focus on the four most relevant milestones that must be in place for the prospect to reach the Revenue Zone.

DEFINING YOUR MILESTONES

Get with your team and review the three key understandings and three key beliefs that define your Revenue Zone and that make up your fifth milestone. Validate that these are still accurate and that, when achieved, will put your prospect squarely in the Revenue Zone. If needed, make any updates in the Builder.

Now work out your other four milestones, in order, that would need to be achieved by your prospect along their path to the Revenue Zone. To help work out these milestones, review past successful sales cycles or any proven processes your company has formulated. Again, speed and simplicity should be the focus. You can always make updates later as you refine and optimize your Yellow Brick Road.

Once you have defined these four additional milestones, add them in the "Five Milestones" tab in the YBR Builder tool.

#	The Five Milestones
1	The prospect has a good understanding of the features and benefits of our accounting software.
2	The prospect believes that these features and benefits will address their specific needs and requirements.
3	The prospect understands how the software will be implemented and the cost and effort associated with the implementation.
4	The prospects believes that this software and company is the best choice compared to other options on the market.
5	THE REVENUE ZONE

YBR Builder - The Five Milestones Tab

At this point, congratulations are in order. You are well on your way to finalizing your Yellow Brick Road. Even just the work you have done so far gives you a huge competitive advantage!

Before you move on to the next step, take a look at the "YBR Journey" tab in the Builder. You should see the framework of your Yellow Brick Road taking place and your five milestones will automatically be displayed. Between each milestone, you will see five numbered rows where each of your bricks will be placed. Let's get going with laying those bricks!

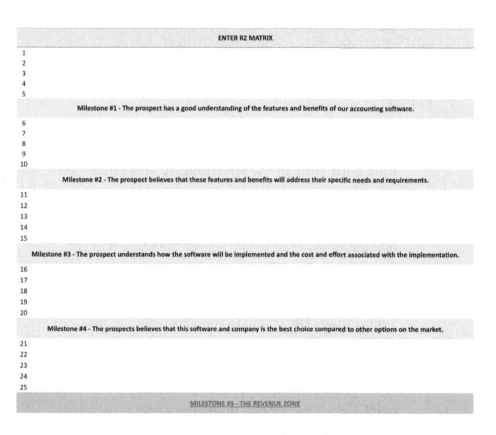

YBR Builder - YBR Journey Tab

SOME QUICK WORDS OF CAUTION...

You may be excited to assemble your internal YBR "construction team" and begin laying the bricks that will ultimately get your prospect into the Revenue Zone. But before you dive in, I have a few suggestions and words of caution:

- **Try to avoid overanalyzing and taking too much time with your brick selections.** At this point, you are simply constructing an initial version of your YBR, and it may be a little rough and even contain a few potholes. That is fine—over time you will constantly be working to make your YBR smoother and better. For now, the most important thing is to get your initial YBR created versus focusing on making it perfect.

- **Don't get bogged down by cracked or missing bricks.** As I mentioned in the last chapter, you will likely find that you are missing critical bricks or that some of your bricks are "cracked" (meaning that they could be out of date, incomplete, or require changes and updates to be made to them).

When you identify missing bricks, please make note of them but then move forward with building the initial version of your YBR using the bricks that you currently have available.

When you identify cracked bricks, you should note that they are in need of repair but go ahead and use them anyway (in whatever shape they are in currently) to build this version of your YBR.

- **Limit yourself to five bricks.** For some milestones, you may find (or believe) that more than five bricks are required to achieve that milestone. When this occurs, you can do two things:

  1. Narrow your selection to the five best bricks you currently have available and note that changes to these bricks may be needed in the future or that new bricks may be required.

  2. Revisit the particular milestone you are working toward and determine if it is too large or in need of refinement so it can be accomplished with five bricks or less.

Whenever possible, I recommend working to select the five best bricks you have available to do the job before revisiting the milestone itself.

- **Prioritize digital bricks.** There will be a tendency (especially with the early milestones) to include bricks that revolve around in-person meetings, product demos, etc. that require the prospect to interact with your sales team. Keep in mind that most prospects want to remain in the Anonymous Zone as long as possible, especially in the early stages of their journey.

  Select bricks that facilitate a "digital first" journey, especially for the early milestones. As the prospect progresses in their journey to the Revenue Zone, you can definitely include bricks that require interaction with your sales team but always ask yourself how a "digital brick" could be utilized to support the prospect whenever possible.

- **Take breaks.** There can be disagreements and quite a bit of emotion that come out as you work through this process. From time to time, some of your team members may feel offended or upset that their suggestions or opinions are not being listened to or accepted.

  Work to keep this process fun and not too serious. Stay focused on the goal of creating your first YBR—which is a really big accomplishment!

I recommend keeping your YBR-building sessions to two hours or less. If you are going to do longer sessions, then make sure to take lots of breaks. Ideally, select your five bricks for a given milestone and then take a break or meet again the next day to focus on the next milestone.

LAYING YOUR BRICKS

Reopen the Builder tool and review Milestone #1. Now, working with your team, identify the top five bricks, in order, that, if followed by the prospect, will result in this first milestone being achieved. Note each brick selected and its order in the "Journey Sequence" column.

Let's go back again to our example of the accounting software company. Their first milestone was *"The prospect has a good understanding of the features and benefits of our accounting software."*

Now let's assume that the following five bricks (that the company previously inventoried and added to their brickyard) were selected as the best options for achieving this first milestone:

1. Website Home Page

2. Product Overview Page

3. eBook: *The Top 5 Features of Modern Accounting Software*

4. Product Overview Video

5. Product Demo Webinar Video

These bricks would have already been added to their Yellow Brick Road Builder tool under the appropriate category during the inventory process. Now the team would simply need to add the number of each brick into the "Journey Sequence" column.

As you add bricks to the journey sequence, you can see everything summarized in the "Yellow Brick Road" tab, and you can watch your overall YBR journey evolving in the "YBR Journey" tab. Pretty cool!

Journey Sequence	Area	Category	Item	Creates Demand	Builds Trust	Potential Impact
1	Online Presence	Website	Home Page	Yes	Somewhat	Positive
2	Online Presence	Website	Product and Services Page	Yes	Yes	Positive
3	Content	Educational	eBook: The Top 5 Features of Modern Accounting	Yes	Yes	Positive
4	Content	Marketing Content	Product Overview Video	Yes	Yes	Positive
5	Content	Marketing Content	Product Demo Webinar Video	Yes	Somewhat	Positive
6	Content	Educational	Customer Case Study Video	Somewhat	Yes	Positive
7	Online Presence	Website	Testimonials	Somewhat	Yes	Positive
8	Online Presence	Review Sites	Customer Reviews on Review Site	Yes	Yes	Positive
9	Content	Marketing Content	Product Data Sheet	Yes	Somewhat	Positive
10	PARTNERS AND INFLUENCERS	PARTNERS	Use Case Blog on Partner Website	Somewhat	Yes	Positive

YBR Builder - Yellow Brick Road Tab

When you are done identifying and adding bricks for Milestone #1, you will simply repeat the same process for Milestone #2, numbering each brick from six to ten.

In our accounting software example, the company's second milestone is *"The prospect believes and understands that these features and benefits can address their needs and requirements."* Their next five bricks to support this milestone could look something like this:

6. Customer Case Study Video

7. Website Testimonials

8. Customer Reviews on Review Site

9. Product Data Sheet

10. Use Case Blog Post on Partner Website

You will then continue this same process for Milestone #3 and Milestone #4. Then you'll select five more bricks that will lead your prospects from Milestone #4 into the Revenue Zone.

When this process is complete, you should see each of the twenty-five bricks that you selected displayed in the "Yellow Brick Road" tab, and your full Yellow Brick Road will be displayed in the "YBR Journey" tab.

ENTER RZ MATRIX	
1	Home Page
2	Product and Services Page
3	eBook: The Top 5 Features of Modern Accounting Software
4	Product Overview Video
5	Product Demo Webinar Video
	Milestone #1 - The prospect has a good understanding of the features and benefits of our accounting software.
6	Customer Case Study Video
7	Testimonials
8	Customer Reviews on Review Site
9	Product Data Sheet
10	Use Case Blog on Partner Website
	Milestone #2 - The prospect believes that these features and benefits will address their specific needs and requirements.
11	
12	
13	

YBR Builder - YBR Journey Tab

GUIDING THE JOURNEY

At this point, you may be wondering how to guide and move your prospect from one brick to the next in the order you defined in your YBR. That is a really good question, especially since we are not likely going to be able to give them an audio guidebook and headphones like my wife and I had at the Boston Museum.

First off, I have found that if you have done a good job creating your YBR sequence, many prospects will naturally follow this route (assuming your YBR bricks are easy to find and identify). We will dig into this more in Chapter 7 when we discuss the Revenue Zone Tech Stack, but you can use website analytics and other tools to monitor how prospects are navigating through your YBR and in what sequence. This data can be used to validate your current YBR and suggest areas for improvement.

Secondly, you can provide recommendations to the prospect on a suggested path they should follow. For example, you could add a button on your website home page guiding the prospect to the next page or action that they should take according to your YBR.

As you validate and optimize your YBR, you want to be constantly looking at how well your bricks are not only providing prospects with the right information at the right time but also how well they are effectively guiding prospects through your YBR.

VALIDATING YOUR YELLOW BRICK ROAD

Once you have defined your YBR, it is a good idea to get other stakeholders in your business (and even your customers) to review and provide feedback. I realize that this can become a tricky process as you may receive a lot of disparate feedback and opinions on the YBR you constructed.

I have found that it is best to treat the feedback you receive as just that—feedback—and to not try to incorporate everyone's suggestions and opinions. Rather, you simply want to use this feedback to validate that the basic framework of your YBR is accurate and that there are no major areas or bricks that you overlooked.

Ideally, you should get feedback from the following stakeholders. You can use the "Yellow Brick Road" and "YBR Journey" tabs in the builder as visual aids in the process.

- Sales and Marketing Team

- Executives

- Partners

- Customers

- Potential Prospects

Once you have received and processed feedback from your stakeholders, you can validate against your initial YBR and, if necessary, make any adjustments. This feedback can also be used as you optimize your YBR going forward.

OPTIMIZING YOUR YELLOW BRICK ROAD

As you no doubt discovered while you were building and validating your YBR, there are areas of your YBR that could be improved and enhanced. You likely also discovered a few missing or cracked bricks that you would like to take care of. What's more, you will likely find as time goes on that your prospects' buying behaviors change over time and that even a perfect YBR can become outdated and require major updates.

As a result, you will need a plan for the ongoing project of optimizing your YBR. Optimizations will generally fall into three categories:

- **Creating new bricks** (across all categories) that will help accelerate and enhance the Buyer's Journey and prospects' experience through the four milestones and into the Revenue Zone.

- **Updating or enhancing existing bricks** that are currently part of your YBR.

- **Updating the sequence and roadmap** you prefer prospects to follow along your YBR.

Whenever possible, use data and analytics to drive your decisions and priorities for optimization rather than letting opinions and subjective ideas rule the day. (We will discuss how to effectively gather and utilize data and analytics in Chapter 7.)

Although you should be continually looking for ways to improve your YBR, try not to make changes and updates too often. Doing so makes your YBR much more difficult to test and validate as your data for each version of the process becomes limited. And when you do make changes, don't make too many all at one time, or you won't be able to know which changes were effective and which were not. (Yes, this is my engineering background coming out…)

TROUBLESHOOTING AND FAQS

Before we end this chapter, I want to take a minute and discuss some common issues you may find with your

Yellow Brick Road and how to address them. I also want to address some frequently asked questions that I receive.

You can also find a complete and up-to-date list of additional troubleshooting tips, tricks, and FAQs at therevenuezone.com/faq. Let's start with a few common YBR issues.

- **Prospects not following your YBR sequence**: Of course, not every prospect is going to follow your exact YBR sequence. However, if you are finding, by reviewing your website analytics and other data, that your sequence is way off track, then you will want to make some adjustments.

  This is best done by reviewing your analytics and understanding what path prospects are following and asking yourself *why* they are following this path. Based on the data you collect about your hypothesis, you can make adjustments to your YBR sequence and continue to monitor the results.

- **Prospects leaving your YBR and not coming back**: First off, remember that the Buyer's Journey is a *journey*—not an event—that can take place over weeks or even months. Also keep in mind that typical

B2B purchases have multiple people involved in the journey, so this can be hard to track and understand.

I will introduce some tools to help with this situation in Chapter 7 as part of the Revenue Zone Tech Stack.

- **Prospects not reaching the Revenue Zone**: Do not expect immediate or overnight success with tons of new prospects flying into the Revenue Zone as soon as you launch your YBR. What we are looking to achieve is a consistently growing number of prospects reaching the Revenue Zone and, over time, the ability to predict how many prospects will end up there.

  There are a number of tools and techniques that I will cover in future chapters to help track and monitor this progress. For now, as you launch and monitor your YBR, stay focused on the sequence and whether prospects are reaching your defined milestones.

In addition to those common issues, here are a few frequently asked questions my team and I often receive. Again, please check out therevenuezone.com/faq for more FAQs and updated recommendations and information.

- **"How do we deal with the fact there are multi-**

ple people involved in the prospect's purchase decision? Should they all be following the same YBR?" Yes, in the early stages of your YBR, you should just define and implement one YBR sequence for all roles and monitor the results. Over time, you may find that you need to create variants of your YBR for some of the different prospect roles (such as for security, IT, etc.), but start with just a single YBR route.

• **"We have many different products and many different types of prospects that we serve. Do we need to create a separate YBR for each product?"** I would recommend that you identify the different product or service *categories* you need to support and build separate YBRs for each disparate category. I would generally not recommend building YBRs for each individual product.

You will likely find there is overlap between your different YBRs and that the same bricks can be used across the YBRs that you create. However, if you're just getting started, please just select one product or service category and get your YBR defined and working properly with that one category before focusing on other categories.

- "A big part of our company's revenue comes from selling more products and services to existing customers. Can the Revenue Zone Matrix and the YBR be used with existing customers?" Glad you asked! Please keep reading, and we will discuss how to successfully generate more consistent sales and drive predictable revenue growth with existing customers in the next chapter.

Chapter Summary

- As you build out your YBR, you are creating a proven process for your prospects to follow in their journey to the Revenue Zone.

- The next step in the YBR process is identifying your four key milestones and entering them into your YBR Builder (therevenuezone.com/ybrbuilder).

- For each milestone, you identify five bricks that, in sequence, will help achieve that milestone.

- As you select your bricks, you update the "Journey Sequence" column in the YBR Builder tool.

- Once you have sequenced all twenty-five bricks in your YBR Builder, you can review your YBR using the "Yellow Brick Road" and "YBR Builder" tabs.

- After your YBR is defined, you should work out how you will guide your prospect from brick to brick.

- You will also want to validate your YBR with key stakeholders in the business and work out a plan for ongoing updates and optimizations.

- Several troubleshooting tips and answers to commonly asked questions are provided at the end of this chapter and at therevenuezone.com/faq.

Discussion Questions

- Who from your company should be involved in defining your YBR?

- Who are good candidates for reviewing and validating your YBR prototype?

- What challenges do you think you will encounter as you define your YBR and how can you address these challenges?

- How can you work through the YBR process quickly without getting stalled or sidetracked?

CHAPTER SIX

THE REVENUE EXPANSION FLYWHEEL

As I mentioned earlier, I grew up in Long Beach, CA and am fortunate enough to still have close relationships with many of my childhood friends, some of whom I have known since kindergarten (which was over fifty years ago—yikes!) One of these long-time friends is Kevin Brown, whom I introduced previously as a significant contributor to the techniques introduced in this book and the overall Revenue Zone philosophy.

Kevin has owned several B2B businesses and is an expert in creating sales and marketing strategies for B2B companies that sell through third-party partners and channels such as distributors, dealers, and resellers. He is also my co-founder at LeadSmart Technologies.

One of the things that Kevin has always stressed to me, as well as to his consulting clients, is the importance of ongoing, repeat sales to existing customers as the focal point of driving predictable revenue growth and profitability in a business. So I knew that Kevin would be my go-to resource and subject-matter expert when I was ready to begin writing this chapter.

In this chapter, we are going to introduce the third and final component of the Revenue Zone System: the Revenue Expansion Flywheel (RE Flywheel). One of the best attributes of the Revenue Zone approach and philosophy is that it inherently lends itself to revenue expansion with existing customers. Once one of your prospects becomes a new customer by purchasing one of your products or services, they then graduate from the Revenue Zone Matrix to the Revenue Expansion Flywheel.

The RE Flywheel is based on "the Flywheel effect" first introduced by Jim Collins and his book *Good to Great*. The premise of the Flywheel is based on the idea of a big, heavy wheel that takes significant effort to get turning but, as you keep pushing, builds more and more momentum until it eventually spins at a nearly unstoppable speed with reduced external effort.

For our purposes, a Flywheel is essentially a self-reinforcing loop driven by a few key initiatives and actions that build on each other and result in immense revenue momentum. This is different from a funnel, where you start at the top and you work your way down. It's also different from the Revenue Zone Matrix, in which you start at the bottom and work your way up.

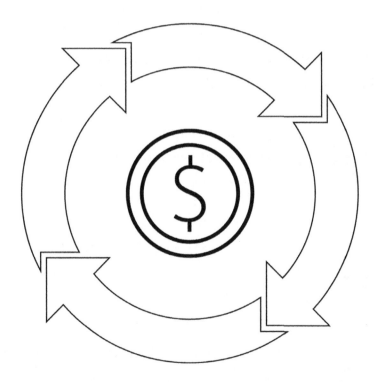

A Flywheel is a Self-Reinforcing Loop

THE REVENUE EXPANSION PLAYBOOK

As you now know, it can take a lot of work and effort to get a prospect through the RZ Matrix and into a paying customer. The good news though is that this effort has already created the initial momentum you need to get your RE Flywheel started, and it is important that you leverage that momentum quickly to keep the Flywheel spinning. Here is the step-by-step playbook that will enable your RE Flywheel to pick up speed and momentum quickly:

1. Give your new customer a remarkable post-sale experience immediately after the sales process is complete (or even before).

2. Leverage the post-sale experience to organically create additional demand for (and sales of) your products and services.

3. Enable your customer to become an ambassador for your products, services, and company.

4. **Rinse and repeat.**

Let's take a look at each of these steps in more detail. Note that each step is an action for you to take. This is to emphasize that none of these steps will just magically happen—they have to be planned out and deliberately implemented.

STEP #1 – COMPLETE THE V3 EXPERIENCE

Congratulations! You just closed (or are close to closing) a new customer. The key to leveraging that momentum and getting your Revenue Expansion Flywheel rolling is providing a great post-sales experience right out of the gate. This is a critical catalyst for getting the Flywheel spinning and, if it is not done well, can pretty much kill any momentum left over from the customer's ascent through the RZ Matrix.

No matter what your new customer purchased, there are

three components of a remarkable post-sale experience, which we call the "V3 Experience":

- **Velocity**: The first part of the V3 Experience is *velocity*. What this means is that you need to provide whatever the customer bought (or if they purchased a service, begin providing) as quickly as possible. For example, if you were to purchase something on Amazon and received it thirty days later, you probably wouldn't consider that such a great experience. That is why Amazon is constantly trying to deliver with more velocity—they want the delivery of the item to be as close to instantaneous as possible.

  The expectations of your new customers, whether they say it or not, are the same. If a new customer has purchased products from your business, make sure they receive or gain access to them (in the case of software or other digital products) with velocity: speed is the name of the game here.

  You need to deliver at least some portion of the service that they purchased or was included in their purchase as quickly as possible, and then continue to deliver the service at a rapid pace.

- **Value**: The next component of the V3 Experience is *value*. What we are looking at here is not just quality but how quickly the customer can start to receive value—and quick wins—from the products or services they have purchased.

  This is different from velocity, which is about how fast you can deliver a product or commence a service. The value component is all about the customer achieving positive outcomes from using the product or service. Work out your "road to value" by mapping out the steps that must be taken for the customer to begin to receive value from your products or services. For some products and services, the road to value is very simple. But for other products and services, it may take some creativity to reduce the time it takes customers to start seeing the results they are looking for. Remember, the customers don't have to get *full value* right at first, but you want them to get at least *some value* as quickly as possible.

- **Validation**: The final component of the V3 Experience is *validation*. Once your customer has started to receive some level of value, you want to look at how that value can be spotlighted within their organization so the person or team who made the buying decision is validated for making a good choice. This can be done by creating a case study that spotlights the customer, sharing their success story on your website, mentioning them in your company's newsletter or social media accounts, or really anything that acknowledges, reinforces, and validates the buying decision and the value now being received from that decision.

The V3 Experience is the catalyst that starts the Revenue Expansion Flywheel. When all three parts of the V3 Experience are in place, you can move on to Step #2.

STEP #2 - CREATE ADDITIONAL DEMAND

An important part of the Revenue Expansion Flywheel (as well as the Revenue Zone Matrix) is understanding the adage, "People love to buy but hate to be sold." In the B2B world, the V3 Experience opens the door for additional sales and revenue expansion without additional "selling." The key to this step working smoothly is having a clear revenue expansion plan and, based on that plan, helping the customer receive more and more value with each additional purchase.

There are generally three types of revenue expansion opportunities that can be included in your plan.

- **Additional consumption:** The customer can buy and consume more of a product or service they have already purchased. For example, assume they purchased a software product for a certain number of users. They could purchase additional user privileges for another part of the company. Or if your company sells construction equipment, maybe your customer bought 100 hard hats originally. They might now need to order 100 more for a different project.

- **Additional products:** your customer might not need any more of the first product they purchased, but they may need something else you offer. If they don't need any more hardhats, perhaps they could use some sledgehammers.

- **Additional services:** even if you aren't primarily a "service provider," you might have an opportunity to sell additional value-add services such as training, consulting, maintenance, or other services related to products your customer has purchased.

If the V3 Experience was completed fully and successfully,

generating additional sales and revenue will be simple. In fact, it will generally happen organically. However, it is important to have a revenue expansion plan for each customer so everyone supporting the customer understands where and when additional value can be added.

STEP #3 - TURN CUSTOMERS INTO RAVING AMBASSADORS

The third part of the Revenue Expansion Flywheel is completely dependent on you executing the previous two steps well. If you use velocity, value, and validation to give your new customer quick wins and then help them with the other needs they have by creating additional demand, your customers will already be willing to be raving ambassadors for your company. Now, let me define exactly what we mean by "ambassador."

An *ambassador* is an individual within the customer's organization who is excited about being a reference for your business. They are willing to actively recommend and promote your products, services, and company to other departments in their own business and, just as importantly, to other companies as well. So, what is a *raving* ambassador?

A *raving ambassador* is someone who is ready to leave a review or provide a sales reference. They are also excited to talk about the V3 Experience they had with your company and can become a key brick in your Yellow Brick Road to support new prospects who enter your RZ Matrix.

One of the most common questions we get asked is whether a company should be willing to financially incentivize an ambassador, and if they should, how to do it. This is a great question, and the right answer for you depends on your situation.

If a customer is being an extraordinary, raving ambassador, then you can definitely look to send special discounts or offers their way. While it is not generally a good idea to financially compensate specific *individuals* within a company, those individuals can be acknowledged and validated in different ways as discussed in the Validation phase of the V3 Experience.

Before continuing with Step #4 of the RE Flywheel process, let's take a minute and look at a real-life example.

THE REVENUE EXPANSION FLYWHEEL IN ACTION

The software company that Kevin and I co-founded back in 2020 is called LeadSmart Technologies. LeadSmart has developed a unique and modern CRM platform that is used predominantly by B2B sales and marketing teams.

In many cases, our customers will initially purchase a limited number of user subscriptions and "pilot" LeadSmart in one or two areas of the company. As a result, we knew early on that getting our RE Flywheel set up and functioning efficiently was key to growing our business. The LeadSmart RE Flywheel process operates as follows:

1. Literally within minutes after the customer agreement is signed, a member of our onboarding team contacts the new customer and schedules a kickoff meeting. We also get a sample LeadSmart environment set up so they can log in and get familiar with the system.

2. During the onboarding meeting, we verify the customer's key needs and requirements and begin the setup process in the CRM. In order to ensure this

happens quickly, our development team has created predefined packages or "apps" that can be installed and configured rapidly. Our goal is to have the LeadSmart system ready for use within days after the kickoff call.

3. Once the setup is complete, we schedule a virtual training session with the new LeadSmart users. The focus of the training is spotlighting the features and capabilities of the system that will help the users generate more sales and revenue quickly. This allows us to demonstrate rapid value and return on investment.

4. A week after the training, we schedule a follow-up meeting with the customer's team to address any questions or issues and, just as importantly, get feedback on the value they are receiving from using the LeadSmart system. We document the "success stories" and share them with other areas of the customer's organization.

The above process incorporates the V3 system by demonstrating velocity, value, and validation. It almost always results in our customers purchasing additional user subscriptions and becoming happy, referenceable ambassadors for our company.

STEP #4 - RINSE AND REPEAT

The RE Flywheel does not end with Step #3. Rather, the secret is to build on the momentum that has already been created and restart the process again—by developing the next V3 Experience, creating more demand, and developing more raving ambassadors.

As you begin to focus on building your Revenue Expansion Flywheel, you will find the Flywheel momentum rapidly increasing on a customer-by-customer basis, and you will create a foundation for consistent sales and ongoing, predictable revenue growth for your company. Not only that, but the RE Flywheel, when properly implemented, will also provide a source of prospects who enter your RZ Matrix with a head start.

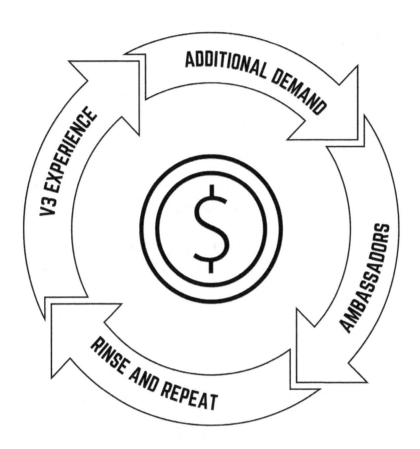

The RE Flywheel

Chapter Summary

- The third and final piece of the Revenue Zone System is the Revenue Expansion Flywheel (RE Flywheel).

- The job of the RE Flywheel is to turn first-time customers into repeat customers, success stories, and references for your company.

- Flywheels require energy to get moving but, when up to speed, continue their powerful momentum with little effort.

- You can generate momentum for your RE Flywheel by:

    1. Creating an extraordinary post-sale experience.

    2. Creating additional demand for your products or services.

    3. Creating raving ambassadors.

    4. Repeating the above process over and over.

- The V3 experience helps create an extraordinary post-sale experience through velocity, value, and validation.

- You can create additional demand for your products and services by targeting additional consumption, additional products, additional services, or any combination of the three.

- Add speed to your RE Flywheel and help move prospects through your RZ Matrix by creating raving ambassadors for your company.

- Continue to build momentum with your RE Flywheel and expand the ongoing revenue associated with each customer by continually repeating this process.

Discussion Questions

- What should the V3 experience look like in your business?

- How can you create additional demand with your customers?

- How can you create raving ambassadors for your company?

- Do you already have ambassadors for your company? (If you do, be sure to include them in your YBR Builder.)

- When your RE Flywheel starts spinning, how will you keep it going? How can you avoid letting it slow down or lose momentum?

CHAPTER SEVEN

THE REVENUE ZONE TECH STACK

Tech Stack (n): A combination of technologies that a company uses to support and/or automate an application, system, or project.

I am a bit of a geek. I first got exposed to computers and computer technology in high school in the early 1980s, and I went on to study technology and computer science in college.

However, I am a bit of an unusual geek in that I am very picky about what technologies I utilize and deploy in my life and my business. My "smart home" is not really all that smart, and I do not have a lot of fancy gadgets or automation around my house. In business, I work to keep my tech stack as lean and efficient as possible. I guess you could say I am a "pragmatic geek."

Now, don't get me wrong: I love technology, and I am fascinated about the future of where technology is headed. However, I also know very well that technology does not always behave like we expect or hope. I also know that some technologies can be very difficult and costly to implement and that support and maintenance can often far exceed the value that the technology brings.

Therefore, it is my belief that each technology in the ideal business tech stack should have the following attributes:

- Has a clear business purpose and helps achieve a clear business objective.

- Is easy to implement, support, and maintain.

- Is easy to use so that others can be trained on it.

- Is able to expand and grow as the business grows.

Yes, I know, this all sounds very pragmatic and not very geeky or exciting. But stay with me. The Revenue Zone Tech Stack (RZ Tech Stack) that I am about to introduce is very powerful and will enable you to take your success with the RZ Matrix, YBR, and RE Flywheel to another level while aligning with the four "pragmatic" attributes listed previously.

OUR GOAL

The first question we need to ask is, "What do we want to accomplish—or what outcome do we want to create—with our RZ Tech Stack?" The right RZ Tech Stack can help you accomplish the following objectives:

- **Know when prospects are active in your RZ Matrix or RE Flywheel.**

- **When possible, know who specifically is active in or who has fallen out of your RZ Matrix or RE Flywheel.**

- **Know if your YBR is effectively guiding prospects to the Revenue Zone or if you need to make adjustments and optimizations.**

- **Track the progress of a prospect in the RZ Matrix and bring them back into the RZ Matrix if they fall out.**

- Automate how you guide and support your prospects in the RZ Matrix and help facilitate them reaching the Revenue Zone.

- Record and track relevant data and information so that you can continually optimize and improve your YBR and help more prospects reach the Revenue Zone.

A FEW ASSUMPTIONS

Before we go much deeper into the specifics of the RZ Tech Stack, I should note that there are a few assumptions I am making about your business and what technologies you currently have in place.

First off, I am assuming you already have a standard website in place that contains information about your company, products, and services.

Second, I am also assuming that you have the standard social media channels set up that make sense for your business, including a Google business profile, YouTube channel, listings on review sites, etc.

Finally, I am assuming that you have the ability to create relevant content such as blog posts, articles, white papers, videos, webinars, podcasts, etc. that make sense for your specific business.

In addition, it is important to note that the RZ Tech Stack is focused on supporting the process after a prospect *enters* the RZ Matrix and is not focused on getting prospects *into* the RZ Matrix. Getting prospects into the RZ Matrix is a topic for a different book.

If you need help establishing your online presence and creating relevant content, please visit therevenuezone.com/partners for recommended companies and consultants who can help you with any of the previously mentioned items.

Okay, enough with the "fine print." Let's get started with setting up your RZ Tech Stack!

THE REVENUE ZONE TECH STACK

There are six technologies that make up the RZ Tech Stack, and we will dig into each layer of the stack in order of importance.

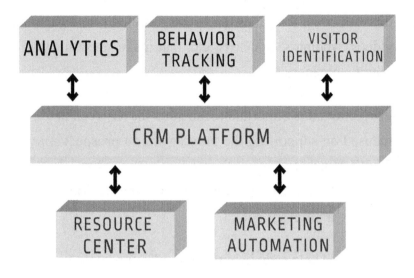

The RZ Tech Stack

#1 - CUSTOMER RELATIONSHIP MANAGEMENT (CRM) PLATFORM

Your CRM Platform is at the heart of the RZ Tech Stack. The purpose of your CRM Platform is to track and manage all the companies and their related contacts that are moving through your RZ Matrix and progressing in your RE Flywheel. It will also act as a central location to track and manage any engagement that takes place with your prospects and customers.

In addition, your CRM Platform should enable you to visualize YBR progress (or lack of progress) through reports, dashboards, and other visualizations. These dashboards and visualizations should help you quickly and easily understand the effectiveness of your RZ Matrix, YBR, and RE Flywheel so that you can make adjustments and optimizations as needed.

Note that I have emphasized your "CRM Platform" versus just a CRM product. The difference is that a CRM Platform enables you to connect and integrate with multiple data sources, including the other technologies in your RZ Tech Stack whereas a CRM product is generally just a place to track accounts, contacts and sales activity. A CRM Platform provides you with a centralized view of everything that is taking place with your prospects and customers.

My software company, LeadSmart Technologies, offers an affordable CRM Platform that has pre-built modules to support your RZ Matrix, YBR, and RE Flywheel. It also integrates with the other technologies in the RZ Tech Stack.

For more recommended CRM Platform options and information, please visit therevenuezone.com/crmplatform.

#2 - RESOURCE CENTER

Your Resource Center lives on your website and is the place where all relevant content that make up your YBR bricks is stored and organized. It can include your own blog posts and articles as well as links to blog posts and articles on other websites, videos, and anything else that is part of your YBR journey.

Your Resource Center should be set up so that each piece of content is easily accessible, organized by relevant categories, and can be searched quickly.

The primary purpose of having a centralized Resource Center is to enable your prospect to find and access the exact content that they need on their YBR journey while keeping them on your own website and not having to search all over the web for the information they need.

Your Resource Center should be organized to fit your specific YBR journey (the one you defined in Chapter 5) as closely as possible.

Some good examples of Resource Centers can be found at therevenuezone.com/resourcecenters.

#3 - MARKETING AUTOMATION

You most likely have some sort of email marketing tool already in place in your business such as Constant Contact, Mailchimp, and others. But the role of your Marketing Automation system in the RZ Matrix and RE Flywheel goes beyond just sending email campaigns. Its primary purpose is threefold:

1. Enable engagement tracking in your email campaigns and track website visitors who engage with your emails.

2. Enable automated follow-up actions to be set up and implemented based on user behavior and actions in your RZ Matrix and RE Flywheel.

3. Send engagement information and details back to your CRM Platform.

My team and I are constantly monitoring and evaluating the different Marketing Automation platforms on the market to find those best able to meet these three requirements. Visit therevenuezone.com/marketingautomation for more information and to see our current Marketing Automation recommendations.

#4 - ANALYTICS

Web Analytics is the process of collecting, measuring, and studying website use data for understanding and improving user experience. Most likely, you have used or seen a web analytics tool such as Google Analytics at one time or another.

Analytics is an important part of your RZ Tech Stack because you want to know how much traffic is coming to your website (especially to your Resource Center), and you want to know if your website visitors (your prospects) are generally following the expected route on your YBR.

Google Analytics is a good choice as an Analytics tool as it allows you to easily view the flow of traffic through each page of your website. It also helps you understand where visitors are leaving your site and how much time they are spending with your content and your YBR bricks.

Visit therevenuezone.com/analytics for examples and more information on how to effectively use Google Analytics on your website. We will also be regularly updating this page as we test and validate new analytics tools that could be alternative options to Google Analytics.

#5 - BEHAVIOR TRACKING

Web Analytics can provide information and data as to *what* is happening in your RZ Matrix, YBR, and RE Flywheel, but it cannot easily help you understand *why* it is happening.

A Behavior Tracking tool working in conjunction with your Web Analytics tool, can help you understand why the behavior is occurring so that you can make the right adjustments to your RZ Matrix or RE Flywheel.

Hotjar is a good and affordable option as a behavior tracking tool. Hotjar helps you graphically map visitor interaction on your various web pages and Resource Center content. You can also set up Hotjar to record visitor actions on your website, which can be very useful for optimizing YBR content. Hotjar also includes capabilities for getting visitor feedback right on your site.

To check out additional Behavior Tracking tools, and to get more details and examples of how to utilize Behavior Tracking on your website, visit therevenuezone.com/behaviortracking.

#6 - VISITOR IDENTIFICATION

The final component of the RZ Tech Stack is Visitor Identification. As you know, your prospects want to stay anonymous as long as possible—until they are ready to make themselves known. A big part of the Revenue Zone philosophy is respecting and supporting this desire and enabling the prospect to remain anonymous and control their own journey.

On the other hand, it is extremely valuable for you to understand (in a non-invasive way) which companies are visiting your website and entering your RZ Matrix. This information will help you understand if you are attracting the right type of prospects and optimize the experience of these prospects throughout your RZ Matrix.

There are a number of Visitor Identification products on the market, including Leadfeeder and Lead Forensics. There are also more comprehensive enterprise options such as 6Sense.

For practicality's sake, it is important that the Visitor Identification product you choose is easy to install and can easily integrate with your CRM Platform. For more information and to check out Visitor Identification options, visit therevenuezone.com/visitoridentification.

REVISITING THE BIGGER PICTURE

Now that you have a better understanding of the RZ Tech Stack components, let's take a look at the bigger picture again.

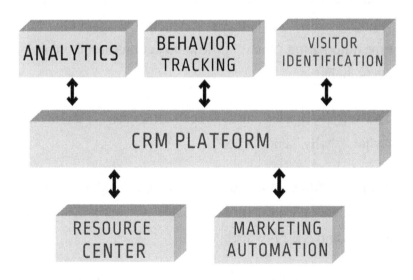

The RZ Tech Stack

Your CRM Platform provides a centralized location for

tracking everything that is taking place with your prospects and customers and for providing insights and intelligence related to your RZ Matrix and RE Flywheel.

Your Resource Center acts as your content hub for all the bricks on your YBR. Its purpose is to make it easy for your prospects to find all the relevant information they need without having to leave your site and bounce around the web.

Your Marketing Automation system helps track prospect engagement with emails and web pages while at the same time automating "smart" follow-up actions based on prospects' behavior.

The top layer of your RZ Tech Stack is all about the "what," "why," and "who."

Your Analytics tool (such as Google Analytics) helps you understand *what* is taking place on your website, RZ Matrix, and RE Flywheel.

Your Behavior Tracking tool enables you to understand *why* these actions and behaviors are taking place so that you can better optimize your YBR and your YBR bricks.

Finally, your Visitor Identification tool helps you understand *who* is in the Anonymous Zone of your RZ Matrix at the company level, so you can be sure that you are bringing the right companies into your RZ Matrix.

Given that technologies are constantly evolving and that new technologies are constantly becoming available, please visit therevenuezone.com/techstack regularly, and my team will keep you up to date with any new changes or developments.

And if you need help with selecting or implementing any of these technologies, we have assembled and qualified a list of consultants and agencies that can assist you. For more information, visit therevenuezone.com/partners.

As I mentioned at the start of this chapter, I am very pragmatic in my use of technology. The RZ Tech Stack reflects that pragmatism. There are probably many other technologies that could be added to the RZ Tech Stack, but I want to make sure that you are not "over-engineering" and are instead keeping your RZ Tech Stack as lean and efficient as possible.

That said, if you find a technology that you think should be included in the RZ Tech Stack, please let us know at therevenuezone.com/techstack, so we can test and evaluate it.

A VALUABLE SIDE EFFECT OF YOUR RZ TECH STACK

As you may recall, in Chapter 1 we discussed the impact that the Privacy Paradigm has made on our ability to make consistent sales and drive predictable revenue growth. The good news is that there is a very valuable "side effect" that you will receive from your Revenue Zone Tech Stack that mitigates this limitation: the ongoing accumulation of first-party data.

Before we continue, let me define what I mean by "first-party data" and how it differs from third-party data.

First-party data is essentially data on businesses and individuals that you collect directly from your prospects and customers. Examples of first-party data include:

- Data from scanning a badge or a business card at a trade show or conference.

- Data from a form on your website.

- Visitor data from your website.

- Customer and purchase information from your e-commerce website.

- Data from quotes, orders, etc.

- Data from tracking a click on a link in an email you sent.

On the other hand, third-party data is data from another website or database outside your organization that you buy (or somehow acquire) access to. Most often, this data is gathered by third-party advertisers like Microsoft, Google, LinkedIn, or Facebook using website cookies and tracking codes. Examples of third-party data use include:

- Using digital ad platforms to create targeted audiences such as "all people that like dogs" or "all businesses that sell hammers." These audiences are being created for your use based on data that come from third-party sources.

- Purchasing an email list for marketing.

- Building digital ad campaigns using interest and demographic targeting (gathered from third-party cookies).

There are a few more nuances to first- and third-party data, but these are the fundamental differences. With the changes and restrictions associated with the Privacy Paradigm, access to third-party data has become increasingly difficult and costly to obtain. However, the good news is that your RZ Tech Stack can provide you with a steady stream of first-party data.

This data can be used to better understand your prospects' behavior, create personalized experiences for your customers, and, when you are ready, drive artificial intelligence and other advanced technologies you may want to work into your marketing and sales efforts in the future.

Even if you are not going to use your first-party data right away, it is important to start capturing it, so that it will be available when you need it.

Your CRM platform will be the primary repository for this data, at least for now, and this data will help us achieve the Tech Stack objectives we outlined at the beginning of this chapter.

Chapter Summary

- A Tech Stack is defined as a combination of technologies that a company uses to support and/or automate an application, system, or project.

- The Revenue Zone Tech Stack is a combination of technologies that will be used to support and automate your RZ Matrix, YBR, and RE Flywheel.

- The RZ Tech Stack is designed to be simple, pragmatic, and focused.

- The RZ Tech Stack contains six key technologies:

  1. CRM Platform - therevenuezone.com/crmplatform

  2. Resource Center - therevenuezone.com/resourcecenters

  3. Marketing Automation - therevenuezone.com/marketingautomation

  4. Analytics - therevenuezone.com/analytics

  5. Behavior Tracking - thereveneuezone.com/behaviortracking

6. Visitor Identification - therevenuezone.com/visitoridentification

- A valuable side effect of your Revenue Tech Stack is that you will be accumulating first-party data about prospects and customers that can be used to continually improve the buyer and customer experience.

- For the latest information and updates related to the RZ Tech Stack, visit therevenuezone.com/techstack.

Discussion Questions

- Why is the Revenue Zone Tech Stack important?

- Why should you try to be as pragmatic and practical as possible about what technologies are included in your RZ Tech Stack?

- Which RZ Tech Stack technologies do you already have in your business? Are they currently being used successfully?

- How can you take advantage of first-party data in your business now or in the future?

CHAPTER EIGHT

MOVING FORWARD: YOUR REVENUE ZONE PLAYBOOK

Let's take a minute and recap what you have accomplished so far (assuming you have been working through each step as you progressed through the book):

1. You know why traditional sales and marketing approaches are outdated and why a change is needed.

2. You understand the Revenue Zone philosophy, approach, and system, and you understand how it will benefit your business.

3. You are familiar with the Revenue Zone Matrix, the Anonymous Zone, the Engagement Zone, and how they relate to prospects reaching the Revenue Zone.

4. You have defined three understandings and three beliefs that your prospects must have in order to reach your Revenue Zone (which is also your fifth milestone in your YBR).

5. You have discovered how the Yellow Brick Road guides prospects into the Revenue Zone and which "bricks" the YBR is made of.

6. You have built your Yellow Brick Road and, by doing so, have created a tailored roadmap for guiding prospects to your Revenue Zone.

7. You understand how the Revenue Expansion Flywheel can drive predictable revenue growth and expansion with your customers.

8. You are familiar with the key components of the Revenue Zone Tech Stack and how they can be used to support your Yellow Brick Road and Revenue Zone Matrix.

Though the foregoing list is impressive and represents substantial progress toward predictable revenue growth for your company in this new era of B2B sales and marketing, you may feel like you're still a few steps away from fully implementing the Revenue Zone System in your business. You may be wondering what specific results you can expect from applying the Revenue Zone and how to measure these results. You may also be hoping for some additional explanation on how to bring everything together and get the most out of the Revenue Zone System in your business.

Not to worry—I have you covered! In this chapter, I will:

- **Provide you with a proven playbook for implementing the Revenue Zone in your business.**

- **Help you define the goals and key performance indicators (KPIs) that will make it easy for you to measure the results and improvements in your business that come from using the Revenue Zone System.**

- **Provide you with options for getting additional help, training, and support.**

THE PLAYBOOK

I define a business playbook as "a go-to approach for getting something done in your business." The playbook that

I am about to give you is designed to help you transition to the Revenue Zone System with minimal disruption and cost to your business while, at the same time, maximizing the results you receive. This playbook for successfully implementing the Revenue Zone in your business involves taking eight steps:

1. Enlighten and educate the key stakeholders in your business on the fundamentals of the Revenue Zone System and the results that it can achieve.

2. Set up your RZ Tech Stack.

3. Select a product or service (or product or service category) that you will use to "pilot" and validate the Revenue Zone System.

4. Build out your RZ Matrix and YBR for your pilot product or service.

5. Launch your RZ Matrix, YBR, and RZ Tech Stack for your pilot product or service.

6. Monitor the results and optimize.

7. Repeat steps 3-6 for additional products and services (if applicable).

8. Implement the RE Flywheel with your customers to drive revenue expansion and predictable revenue growth.

Let's take a look at each of these steps in more detail.

STEP #1 - ENLIGHTEN AND EDUCATE KEY STAKEHOLDERS

If you have a smaller company, there may be just a handful of key stakeholders that you need to work with. Or if you have a larger business, you may need to enlighten and educate many different people on the Revenue Zone System and its benefits.

Generally, the relevant stakeholders consist of sales and marketing executives and certain C-level executives who are actively involved in sales and revenue generation. You may also need to do some education with your IT team as part of setting up your Revenue Zone Tech Stack.

The key topics that you want these stakeholders to have at least a minimal understanding of are:

- *Why* they would want to implement the Revenue Zone in their business and the potential consequences of continuing with traditional sales and marketing approaches (as covered in the introduction and Chapter 1).

- *How* the Revenue Zone is different from other sales and marketing approaches in terms of its philosophy and underlying mindset (as covered in Chapter 2).

- *What* the Revenue Zone Matrix is and how it differs from traditional sales funnels and processes (as covered in Chapter 3).

I have found that the best way for stakeholders to get enlightened and educated on the above items is to quickly read (or listen to) the introduction and Chapters 1-3 of this book (if not the entire book). This approach works much better than trying to explain the Revenue Zone System in a presentation or slide deck.

If you would like free PDF copies of the introduction, Chapter 1, Chapter 2, and Chapter 3, or would like to order additional copies of the full Revenue Zone book or audio book for your team and stakeholders at discounted pricing, please go to therevenuezone.com/materials.

STEP #2 – SET UP YOUR REVENUE ZONE TECH STACK

How you take the next step will depend on what parts of the RZ Tech Stack you already have running in your business. Although you may have some or all of the RZ Tech Stack technologies in place, you will need to configure them in accordance with the Revenue Zone objectives.

Your RZ Tech Stack can be configured in two phases based on. Your Phase 1 implementation should include:

- The CRM Platform

- The Resource Center

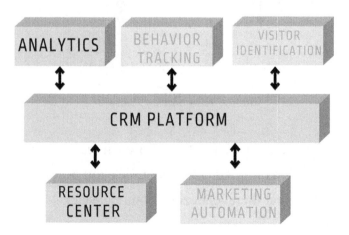

The RZ Tech Stack - Phase 1

- Analytics

Once you have the above three technologies up and running, you can focus on Phase 2, which will include:

- Marketing Automation

- Behavior Tracking

- Visitor Identification

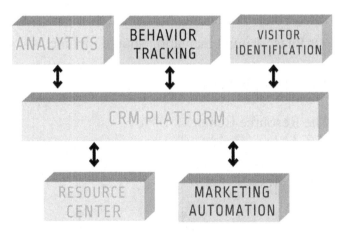

The RZ Tech Stack - Phase 2

Recommended product options for each technology category as well as implementation guides and best practices can be found at therevenuezone.com/techstack.

If you need help selecting or implementing any of these

technologies, please reach out using the Contact Form on our Tech Stack web page (therevenuezone.com/techstack), and we can help provide you with options that make sense for your business.

Note: You do not need to have your RZ Tech Stack set up and fully functional to continue with the next few steps of the playbook. However, it is a good idea to have your technologies selected and the implementation process underway so that you are ready to launch when you reach Step #5.

STEP #3 - SELECT A "PILOT" PRODUCT OR SERVICE

Implementing the Revenue Zone System with just a single product or service (for starters) is a means to stay focused and convince stakeholders of the system's effectiveness by demonstrating tangible results before expanding into other areas.

The specific product or service you select as your "pilot" will depend on your business and the types of products or services you sell. Here are some general guidelines that

I recommend you take into consideration when making your decision:

- Select an established product or service that is already having some level of success in the market. This will enable you to convincingly compare "before and after" stats and metrics. In addition, there are generally other go-to-market issues and challenges related to launching a new product or service, which can get in the way of successfully piloting the Revenue Zone System. The Revenue Zone System is a great way to launch a new product or service, but new products or services are not recommended for the pilot.

- Select a product or service for which you already have active marketing campaigns in place that are generating a good number of new leads and prospects. This makes it much easier to get a good number of prospects into your Revenue Zone Matrix and moving along your Yellow Brick Road. More prospects means more data and clearer results.

- Select a product or service that already has "bricks" in place that you can use to construct your Yellow Brick Road. This makes implementation faster and less costly.

- Select a product or service that is supported by a sales and marketing team that understands the Revenue Zone approach and is excited to pilot and validate the system.

STEP #4 - BUILD OUT THE REVENUE ZONE MATRIX AND YELLOW BRICK ROAD FOR YOUR PILOT

Now that you have selected your pilot, take a minute and revisit Chapter 3, this time with your pilot product or service in mind. Then continue on by using the YBR Builder tool (available at therevenuezone.com/ybrbuilder) and following the step-by-step process outlined in Chapter 4 and Chapter 5.

STEP #5 - LAUNCH THE REVENUE ZONE MATRIX, YELLOW BRICK ROAD, AND TECH STACK FOR YOUR PILOT

Okay, now is the time to launch your Revenue Zone System. But what does that mean exactly?

By "launch" I simply mean you are moving prospects into your RZ Matrix and YBR and tracking results. You can drive prospects into the RZ Matrix using whatever marketing and lead generation campaigns and actions make sense for your business. Congratulations, your Revenue Zone System is live!

STEP #6 - MONITOR RESULTS AND OPTIMIZE

If you've followed the steps up to this point, then you should have prospects moving into your Revenue Zone Matrix and—hopefully—moving along your Yellow Brick Road toward the Revenue Zone.

Now is the time to use your RZ Tech Stack to monitor and track your prospects' progress. After a few weeks, you'll know whether your Revenue Zone System is working and if there are any issues.

If there are issues (which is frequently the case with pilots), adjust and optimize your Yellow Brick Road as needed. Be sure to use the data provided from your RZ Tech Stack to evaluate progress and make decisions; don't just guess or rely on opinions and hope for the best.

Continue monitoring and optimizing until you are seeing consistent results and a steady stream of prospects moving through your four milestones and into your Revenue Zone.

STEP #7 - REPEAT STEPS 3-6 FOR ADDITIONAL PRODUCTS OR SERVICES

If you only have one primary product or service, then you can skip this step and move on to Step #8. But if you have other products or services (or product or service categories) you should now look at repeating steps 3-6 for each major product or service you offer.

If you have many products or services, you may want to implement the Revenue Zone with more than one product or service at a time. This is fine if you feel confident with the RZ Matrix and YBR and if your RZ Tech Stack is functioning well and providing you with good data and insights. Otherwise, I recommend that you repeat steps 3-6 using one product or service at a time.

STEP #8 - IMPLEMENT THE REVENUE EXPANSION FLYWHEEL WITH EXISTING CUSTOMERS

Unless your business generates a large percentage of revenue from existing customers, I recommend that you focus on optimizing your RZ Matrix and YBR before implementing the RE Flywheel. But if existing customers are responsible for a larger portion of your sales and revenue, or if you have successfully implemented your RZ Matrix and YBR, you should definitely turn your attention to setting up and turning on your RE Flywheel.

Start by defining and really nailing the V3 Experience for new customers as outlined in Chapter 6. Then work out which follow-up products and services would provide the most value to your customers. Finally, work out how to spotlight the success of your customers and create raving ambassadors (see Chapter 6).

By taking these eight steps, you will successfully implement the Revenue Zone System in your business. Remember, as I mentioned previously, that this is a journey and not an event, so please do not be discouraged or lose faith if you do not see immediate results. Just keep following the eight steps outlined here. My promise is that you will ultimately see results and create a huge competitive advantage for your business.

MEASURING RESULTS - GOALS AND KPIS

One of the strengths of the Revenue Zone System is that it can be monitored, tracked, and optimized using data and analytics. So, what data, analytics, and key performance indicators (KPIs) should you be tracking?

I like to keep this as simple as possible (do you see a theme developing here?). Here are the primary goals that I recommend that you set and seek to monitor:

1. Maintain an ever-growing number of prospects moving into the Revenue Zone.

2. Maintain a high percentage of Revenue Zone prospects turning into customers.

3. Keep existing customers buying more products and services and generating ongoing revenue streams for the business.

With those goals in mind, here are the primary KPIs that you will want to monitor using your CRM Platform and your other RZ Tech Stack tools:

- Number of prospects entering the RZ Matrix.

- Number (and percentage) of prospects reaching Milestone #1.

- Number (and percentage) of prospects reaching Milestone #2.

- Number (and percentage) of prospects reaching Milestone #3.

- Number (and percentage) of prospects reaching Milestone #4.

- Number (and percentage) of prospects reaching the Revenue Zone (Milestone #5).

- Number (and percentage) of Revenue Zone prospects turning into customers.

If you want to get more advanced with your KPIs, you can also measure the average time duration that it takes for a prospect to move from one milestone to the next or through the entire process.

I would recommend tracking these KPIs using weekly metrics on a dashboard in your CRM Platform so you can visually see the impact of changes and improvements you make to your system. Examples of sample dashboards and visualizations can be found at therevenuezone.com/crmplatform.

These KPIs are the foundation for achieving predictable revenue growth and for monitoring the ongoing success of your Revenue Zone System. What you want to see, over time, is continual increases in these KPIs and improvements in the three goals being achieved. While there will certainly be ups and downs from week to week, if you find that a specific KPI is continually getting worse, you should debug and optimize as needed.

GETTING ADDITIONAL HELP AND SUPPORT

We have covered a tremendous amount of ground in this book, and you may feel that you need some additional help with using and successfully implementing the Revenue Zone System in your business. You may also want to see some more real-world examples and case studies related to the RZ Matrix, YBR, RE Flywheel, or RZ Tech Stack.

I totally get it! My team and I have assembled (and are continually updating) a comprehensive online resource center that you can access for free at therevenuezone.com/resources. No signup or membership is required to access the RZ Resource Center, but I highly recommend that you register so you receive notifications when new resources are added or major updates occur.

Here is a quick tour of what you can expect to find in the RZ Resource Center:

- **News and Articles (therevenuezone.com/news).** Stay up to date on research and news from industry leaders and experts related to changes that are taking place in B2B sales and marketing and the potential impact these changes will have on your business.

- **Yellow Brick Road Builder Tool (therevenuezone. com/ybrbuilder).** Access the YBR Builder tool and get more detailed instructions (including instructional videos) on how to successfully utilize the Builder.

- **Frequently Asked Questions (the revenuezone. com/faq).** Browse a growing list of common questions (and answers!) related to all aspects of the Revenue Zone System and its implementation.

- **Case Studies and Examples (therevenuezone. com/examples).** Access case studies and examples from other businesses that are implementing the Revenue Zone principles. You can also share your own experience here.

- **The Revenue Zone Tech Stack (therevenuezone. com/techstack).** Get more information, recommendations, and implementation strategies related to all aspects of the RZ Tech Stack.

- **Training and Certification (therevenuezone.com/ training).** Expand your knowledge of the Revenue Zone through courses and other training (including certification as a Revenue Zone specialist).

- **Partners (therevenuezone.com/partners).** Use our growing list of Revenue Zone partners to connect with people who can help you take full advantage of the Revenue Zone System and technologies in the RZ Tech Stack. You can also apply to become a Revenue Zone partner here.

- **Materials (therevenuezone.com/materials).** Grab free PDF versions of the introduction and chapters 1,2 and 3 as well as order copies of the Revenue Zone book and/or audio book for your company at special wholesale prices.

- **Digital Advertising/Paid Media (therevenuezone. com/paidmedia).** At the time of publishing, there were several new and innovative options in digital advertising and paid media that were just released by Google and others that appear to be a perfect complement and accelerator for any YBR. Visit our paid media page for the latest-and-greatest digital advertising and paid media strategies that will help you turbo charge your RZ Matrix and YBR.

- **Work with Us (therevenuezone.com/workwithus).** - Find out how you can work directly with me and my team, so we can help you design and implement the ultimate Revenue Zone System in your business.

- **And More!** My team and I will continually be adding new categories and information to the RZ Resource Center, so be sure to subscribe to notifications to get the latest updates.

FINAL THOUGHTS

Back in the introduction to this book, I boldly stated that "what got us *here* will not get us *there*."

The purpose of this book—and the Revenue Zone System in general—is to ensure that you and your business "get there" and are making consistent sales and driving predictable revenue growth in this next generation of B2B sales and marketing.

But even more importantly, once you're "there," you will be building strong and trusting relationships with your prospects and customers and eliminating any chasms or rifts that have been created by old-school sales and marketing techniques.

Personally, I would really like to see the Gartner statistics that I presented in the introduction to flip flop. I want to see that prospects and buyers are totally willing to engage with sales teams and welcome guidance and support as part of their Buyer's journey. When that happens, we'll know the world has embraced and understands the power of the Revenue Zone.

Let's make it happen!

Chapter Summary

- A business playbook provides you with a "go-to approach for getting something done in your business."

- The Revenue Zone Playbook consists of eight steps:

  1. Enlighten and educate key stakeholders.

  2. Set up your Revenue Tech Stack.

  3. Select a "pilot" product or service.

  4. Build out the RZ Matrix and YBR for your pilot.

  5. Launch.

  6. Monitor results and optimize.

  7. Repeat steps 3-6 for additional products or services.

  8. Implement the RE Flywheel with customers.

- Use goals and KPIs to monitor the progress of your prospects and the results your Revenue Zone System produces.

- The Resource Center (therevenuezone.com/resources) is a comprehensive source for additional help and support with your Revenue Zone implementation.

Discussion Questions

- Which stakeholders in your business should learn more about the Revenue Zone?

- Who in your organization should be involved in implementing the Revenue Zone by taking the eight playbook steps?

- What goals and KPIs are most important for your business?

- What help and support from the Resource Center might your company need?

- How do you hope your business' relationship with prospects and customers will change by implementing and adopting the Revenue Zone?

GLOSSARY

Here is a glossary of Revenue Zone terminology in the order that it was introduced in the book. Related abbreviations for each term are shown in parentheses.

- **The Revenue Zone®**: The official title of this book.

- **Revenue Zone Resource Center**: The online location of Revenue Zone related resources and tools (therevenuezone.com/resources) that are used in conjunction with this book.

- **The Revenue Zone System™ (RZ System)**: Collectively, the philosophies, strategies and techniques presented in The Revenue Zone book.

- **Revenue Zone**: A place in the buyer's journey that they are seriously considering spending money on your products or services. It is also the primary destination of the Revenue Zone Matrix and Yellow Brick Road.

- **Yellow Brick Road™ (YBR)**: Represents the most successful "route" that a prospect would follow to reach the Revenue Zone in the shortest amount of time. It is composed of "bricks" and "milestones."

- **Revenue Zone Matrix™ (RZ Matrix)**: A unique framework and matrix designed to move as many prospects as possible into the Revenue Zone.

- **Anonymous Zone**: The first area or section in the Revenue Zone Matrix where the prospect is working to stay incognito and anonymous while doing their research and due diligence.

- **Engagement Zone**: The second area or section in the Revenue Zone Matrix where the prospect is working willing to engage and communicate with your sales team (or other appropriate person) in your company.

- **Yellow Brick Road Builder (YBR Builder)**: A special online, interactive tool that can be used to organize your "bricks" and Yellow Brick Road route.

- **Bricks**: Represents a specific step or event in your Yellow Brick Road journey (which is composed of 25 total bricks).

- **Milestones:** A significant point that is reached in the Yellow Brick Road that results in a prospect achieving an understanding and/or a belief. There are five total milestones in the Yellow Brick Road (the fifth being the Revenue Zone).

- **Revenue Expansion Flywheel™ (RE Flywheel)**: A self-reinforcing loop driven by prescribed actions (as described in Chapter 6) that build on each other and result in revenue expansion with existing customers.

- **Revenue Zone Tech Stack (RZ Tech Stack)**: A combination of specific technologies that are used to support and/or automate the Revenue Zone System.

- **Revenue Zone Playbook (RZ Playbook)**: The "go to" approach and method for implementing the Revenue Zone System in your business.

ENJOY THIS BOOK?

Order a copy for a friend or colleague today on Amazon or at therevenuezone.com!

You can also connect with Tom on social media for the latest Revenue Zone updates, tips, and tools in this next generation of sales, marketing, and predictable revenue growth.

LinkedIn: tburton5350
Twitter: @tomburtonsb

Scan for Digital Business Card

Made in the USA
Middletown, DE
25 June 2022

67574423R00116